Paper Genders

*Pulling the Mask Off
the Transgender Phenomenon*

Walt Heyer

Make Waves
PUBLISHING

PAPER GENDERS

ISBN: 978-1-7323453-2-4

Written by Walt Heyer

Cover design by Tia Ramey
rameymarketing.com

Edited by Kaycee Heyer
Interior layout by Kaycee Heyer

Publishing by Make Waves Publishing

Second printing June, 2011
Third printing January, 2020

Table of Contents

❧

Dedication

To all those who suffer disappointment or regret
after beginning a gender transition or undergoing
radical genital surgery.

To those who unfortunately have ended their own
lives because changing gender did not deliver the
emotional relief that was promised.

To their families, who hurt along with their
loved ones.

Foreword

You can tell the character of a person by seeing how their life story is lived out. Stories travel many different roads, up and down, with twists and turns. Those roads include tragedy and joy, beauty and ashes, encouragement and despair. How one deals with these hairpin turns of life determines one's character.

If you have read Walt's previous books, you know his story is, by many accounts, tragic. Yet at this point in that journey, washed in the power and grace of God Himself, stands a man of honor, a husband of respect, a father of commitment. For Walt it has created a man of rigorous honesty and integrity, a man of vulnerability and acute insight and determination.

This book is a sacrificial product of the desire to tell whole truths. He pens his exhaustive research with personal experience of "been there, done that." You may not agree with what he has to say but for your own intellectual honesty, read before you become one who says, "Do not confuse me with the facts; my mind is already made up!" Walt's intellectual integrity flows from his life into his words.

It is with a thankful prayer that I have met such a man who, from a knock on our door as a stranger some twenty-five years ago, has become one of our best friends.

—*Roy Thompson, PhD*

Introduction

This book was not encouraged in any way, verbally or financially, in full or in part, by any organization, activist group, and/or movement, including any and all political groups and/or church affiliations of any kind whatsoever. This book was compelled by my own personal experience which has been lived out in stark contrast to the overwhelming glamorization of gender change success by the media and activist groups.

Changing genders results in far too many suicides and irreparably damaged or destroyed lives. For a long time I have seen all kinds of evidence that points in that direction. I have waited in vain for the media and activists to come clean and I came to see that, as improbable as it seemed, the task of pulling together the facts of the blotted history and negative outcomes of gender change fell to me.

This book was motivated only by my personal desire to help transgenders by shining light on the dark side of changing genders. I feel I have done that.

Now a word about who this book is for. Gender identity disorders are complex and not fully understood. I think researchers will eventually find that the symptom of wishing to identify as the opposite gender originates from many disparate medical and psychological issues, rather than a one-size-fits-all diagnosis.

Some of those who suffer from gender identity issues feel caught in an intense internal battle. To attain temporary relief from the emotional pressure boiling inside, they turn to what might seem an unusual way to cope—they express themselves outwardly as the opposite gender. The feelings are far too strong and continuous and for that reason those who experience them are unable to just stuff them away out of sight, like most of us would like to see them do. The outward expression is the only way sufferers can communicate their gender identity feelings. Often the outward expression progresses from cross-dressing once in a while to taking cross-gender hormones; from taking hormones to living as the opposite gender; and to the last step, undergoing surgery to irreversibly modify their genitals. Unfortunately, many regret the gender surgery and return to living in their birth gender, now feeling lost and stuck with the wrong genitalia.

Gender switchers should not be faced with scorn or subject to abuses just because we lack understanding of their suffering. However in, my view, we do need to provide them room for expression without resorting to surgical intervention unless absolutely necessary. They do need more help in preventing suicide and regret, including capable medical and psychological professionals to help them through this excruciating conflict that evolves into a gender identity crisis.

It is my desire that this book will provide a new understanding and serve as a guide to preventing transgender suicides.

Chapter 1.

Gender, Lies and Suicide

They commit suicide at a rate reported to be nearly 10 times greater than the general population. They struggle psychologically and emotionally with strong feelings and feel driven to change their appearance through extensive plastic surgery. They undergo months, even years, of hormone treatments and as the ultimate endpoint, they surgically rearrange their genitalia. Today some women you see about town are actually *men* and some who look like men are actually *women*. They are commonly referred to as gender variant, transsexual or transgender. (But not the same as intersex, born with both male and female genitalia; this physical condition is not related in any way to transsexualism.[1])

The media calls the transsexual surgical procedure "sex change surgery," but the term is misleading because it is impossible to change anyone's birth gender with cosmetic surgery and hormones. On paper, though, the change can be made with ease and in fact, that's the only place where sex change occurs, on birth certificates and driver's licenses.

Unfortunately, many regret the gender change years after the surgery, but you would never learn that from the media. For years they have bombarded us with stories, infomercials really, that glamorize gender switching, while neglecting to report the high suicide attempt rate, suicide completion rates and high overall mortality that has occurred as a direct result of gender surgery.

Their cover is now blown.

A survey of more than 7,000 transgender people released in October, 2010, found:

> *That 41 percent suicide rate among transgender people is more than 25 times the rate of the general population, which is 1.6 percent. And among trans people ages 18-44, the suicide attempt rate was 45 percent.*[2]

A web site whose mission is to "lower the horrendous suicide rate and provide online support for all Transgendered persons and their families" makes the following mortality estimate based on crisis calls over a five-year period:

> *Based on conversations with 9 million users and over 2 million emails I'd estimate the total Transgender mortality rate at between 60% to 70% and I'm being conservative...*[3]

The same site speaks to the difficulty in estimating transgender mortality:

> *Transgender mortality rates are difficult to estimate because families often don't report that there (sic) dead son or daughter was transgender. In addition deaths due to illegal hormone use and its complications aren't reported because they don't seek a doctor's help. Common problems are strokes, heart attacks, silicone injections and deep vein thrombosis. There are also thousands of cases of unreported violence leading to death.*[4]

A different transgender support site talks about transgender suicide:

The National suicide rate is 3 per 100,000 People. The Transgender Transsexual suicide rate is 31% of our group. Over 50% of Transsexuals will have had at least one suicide attempt by their 20th birthday. Even more self harm themselves daily either by cutting or self mutilation.

Between 90-95 percent of people who attempt suicide are suffering from some sort of mood disorder or substance use disorder.[5]

The gender change activists would argue the suicides are a direct result of bullying, a popular scapegoat these days. The advocates also say the lack of transgender acceptance and the difficulty of being gender variant in a society of heterosexuals lead to suicides, but as the last transgender support site disclosed, transgenders harm *themselves* either by cutting or self-mutilation, which points to deep unresolved psychological issues.

Estimates of transgender suicides attempts vary widely, from 20 to 50%, depending on the study group and geographic location of the study. (Government sources do not track transgender statistics.) But no matter where in the range it falls, the high death rate should alarm us all and be the positive proof that switching of genders is neither safe nor effective as a treatment for gender disorders or depression.

When I first became aware of the suicide rate, I wanted to know why, especially since gender change is portrayed as being the best treatment for this population. What was found was troubling, shocking and very alarming.

Alfred Kinsey

To discover how this all started we go back to 1948, with the publication and ensuing popularity of the book *Sexual Behavior in the Human Male* by Dr. Alfred Kinsey. Even though the book was full of charts and made for dry reading, 185,000 copies were sold in the first year alone, making it a best-seller.[6] That book, together with Kinsey's second book, *Sexual Behavior in the Human Female* (1953), commonly became known as *The Kinsey Reports* and sparked what came to be known as the sexual revolution.

What shocked America were his statistics. For example, Kinsey declared that 37% of American males had engaged in a homosexual experience and nearly 47% reported having feelings toward the same sex during their life. Under the guise of scientific research, Alfred Kinsey set in motion a significant shift in U.S. social history by validating and mainstreaming homosexuality and other sexual practices. His methodology was not sound, but that wouldn't be found out until much later.

The media was very good to Kinsey. Dr. Judith Reisman, researcher and author of the 1998 exposé, *Kinsey: Crimes & Consequences,* says in her 1998 interview with *The New American:*

> *...the sympathetic national media...accepted and promoted the Kinseyan legal and scientific claims without question. Kinsey was on the cover of most of our magazines and was celebrated in newspaper headlines and television news stories as a great scientist who was freeing the world from our unhealthy, puritanical sex repressions.* [7]

But the reality was far different. Kinsey from a young age, in the words of Reisman, was a "violently masochistic masturbation addict" and a sexual predator.[8] His perverted predilection started at age seven in a neighborhood basement with other kids. According to his brother, as a teen Kinsey hid out in the attic masturbating and using various tools to inflict pain on his penis. His sexual addiction progressed from masturbation addict to world-class sexual predator and bully who preyed on adults and children alike for his own sadistic pleasure and labeled it research.[9]

Kinsey was a strong advocate of pedophilia and for eliminating laws that protected children from engaging in sex with adult men. One of Kinsey's male sex partners directed the primary sex accrediting institute in the USA which published a photographic book that included child pornography called *Meditations on the Gift of Sexuality*.[10] Dr. Reisman says,

> *Kinsey believed that all sex was legitimate— pedophilia, bestiality, incest, adultery, prostitution, group sex, transvestitism, sadomasochism—and he worked to overthrow all laws prohibiting any of these perversions.* [11]

Harry Benjamin

In 1945, Alfred Kinsey was introduced to Dr. Harry Benjamin, an endocrinologist in New York. Their friendship included some professional collaboration, as Dr. Benjamin says in a 1985 interview:

> *I met Kinsey in New York through the well-known American gynecologist R. L. Dickinson sometime around 1945. Three years later in San Francisco, he lived in the same hotel as I did - the Sir Francis Drake. I had, in the meantime, opened a second (i.e., summer) practice right across from this hotel (in the Sutter Medical Building at 450 Sutter Street.*

> *Kinsey came to California quite often because of his interviews, and he asked my advice in the case of a boy he had met on one of these occasions. This very effeminate boy wanted, as he said, to become a girl, and his mother supported him in this. Kinsey had never seen a case like this, and it was new even for me. This case looked to go*

well beyond the then recognized transvestism. The concept of transsexualism did not yet exist; it only gradually took shape in my thinking, not least because of this first case. I introduced the term only in 1954, and my book on the subject did not appear until 1966 (The Transsexual Phenomenon).

Anyway, I asked for the boy's psychiatric examination under the aspect of possible surgery that would make his body more female in appearance. The psychiatrists disagreed among themselves. Some were for it, others against it.

However, the boy received "female" hormones that "had a calming effect". He then travelled to Germany, where he underwent partial surgery. After that, I unfortunately lost contact with him, and thus I do not know what ultimately became of the case. [12]

Dr. Harry Benjamin agreed with Kinsey's views of pedophilia. What is the evidence? Benjamin and Kinsey were close friends with René Guyon, a prominent, acknowledged pedophile.[13] Benjamin endorsed Guyon's 1948 book, *The Ethics of Sexual Acts*, which advocates the normalcy and decriminalization of behaviors such as sex abuse against children. The endorsement reads:

Writing an introduction to a new edition of a book by Rene Guyon is a signal honor...There is hardly an author anywhere with qualifications comparable to those of Guyon... [14]

You would think a person wouldn't lend his name to a book unless he wholeheartedly endorsed the content.

Dr. Benjamin's work with the treatment of transgenders was experimental, of course. His theory was that the gender the patient *desired* was correct, and their body parts were wrong. Therefore, it followed that the solution was to treat the patient with hormones and cosmetic surgery to help correct that wrong. Benjamin provided the hormone treatment and carefully selected colleagues of various disciplines to assist, such as psychiatrists, electrologists (for hair removal), and plastic surgeons.[15]

John Money

Benjamin's work as a sexologist was familiar to another colleague, Dr. John Money (1921–2006), a professor of pediatrics at John Hopkins University, a psychologist, sexologist, author and well known for his research into sexual identity. Dr. Money was a dedicated Kinsey disciple and served on the advisory board of the Kinsey Institute. Money co-founded the Johns Hopkins Gender Identity Clinic. [16]

Money will be remembered most notably for moving the topic of sex change surgery from quiet whispers around company water coolers, to mainstream America and the headlines of news outlets around the country.

Once again, in looking at the founders whose practice was treating gender disorders, we'll see that character matters. Just like Kinsey and Benjamin, Dr. Money advocated pedophilia. A common thread among the founders of gender changing is that they all actively promoted the decriminalization of child abusers. As *Time Magazine* reported on April 14, 1980:

> *Says John Money of Johns Hopkins, one of the best-known sex researchers in the nation: "A childhood sexual experience, such as being the partner of a relative or of an older person, need not necessarily affect the child adversely."* [17]

In a 1991 interview with the pedophile periodical, *The Journal of Pedophilia*, Professor Emeritus Dr. John Money offered his professional opinion about men having sex with boys:

> *If I were to see the case of a boy aged ten or eleven who's intensely erotically attracted toward a man in his twenties or thirties, if the relationship is totally mutual, and the bonding is genuinely totally mutual...then **I would not call it pathological in any way** (emphasis added).* [18]

John Money produced pornography in the name of science and education. Dr. Judith Reisman, in her exposé, *Kinsey: Crimes & Consequences,* put it this way:

> *As a professor, he compiled an illustrated presentation called "Pornography in the Home," which became very popular with students at Johns Hopkins Medical School. Since Johns Hopkins enjoyed a leadership role among American medical colleges it is not surprising that [roughly 90% of] medical schools followed its lead in initiating explicitly sexual pornography films as part of the curriculum for their students.* [19]

The pedophile connection is very difficult to ignore with Dr. Alfred Kinsey followed by Dr. Harry Benjamin, then Dr. John Money, the co-founder of the Johns Hopkins Gender Identity Clinic. All three men, it appears, did not advocate for any other therapies, only for the freedom to switch genders. They set out to redefine how men and women were made and for them it was not in the womb. The agenda was always about freedom to select a new gender.

The media ink spilled into the mix. On October 4, 1966, a gossip column in the *New York Daily News* carried the astounding story about a beautiful woman who frequented the clubs and claimed to have been a male a year before. Her surgery had been performed at Johns Hopkins, the most prestigious medical center in the world. The story was printed in *The New York Times* as well as newspapers across the country. Dr. Money's surgical gender changing had gone coast to coast. It was Dr. John Money, along with his team of surgeons, who would start a trend in switching genders that would redefine male and female.[20]

The news in 1966 did two things. First, everyone reading the news thought it was true, that surgery could change a male into a female. Second, Dr. John Money must be a brilliant guy. Neither was true. Dr. John Money was able to bring about what could be the greatest medical fraud in history. He delivered what he said was "sex change" surgery to mainstream America. This man's ego could not be contained. Later, the term sex change was replaced with gender reassignment. Let's call it paper genders because the only change is on paper—birth certificate, driver's license, and so forth.

When you tell a lie often enough people start to think it is true. Just the statement "A surgeon and a knife can change a man into a woman" is a bit presumptuous on its own. When you realize it cannot be done, you can only laugh your way into hysteria, except it is not funny when so many die. We have become so accustomed to looking the other way at crazy things we see on television. We look but ask no serious questions.

It's easy to point out that DNA tells the true story of male or female. In a court of law, you can convict a man of rape and murder just on the strength of a DNA test alone. But a DNA test is never permitted to determine male or female sex gender for transsexuals in court. Why is this? Because a DNA test would prove with absolute certainty the transgender hormone therapy and surgery *had failed* to change a male to a female, or a female to a male. Transgender activists know using DNA would expose the fraud and damage the social acceptability of changing genders. Therefore, they have successfully prevented DNA from being used as the criteria to identify gender in the courts.

The court which displays "In God we trust" allows transgenders to *legally amend original birth records* to reflect a change in gender even though it is not physically possible. Amazing freedom is afforded transgenders in court. Perhaps we should see "In transgenders we trust" printed on the wall above the judge.

Allowing the original birth record gender to be altered has unintended consequences. It can be misused, perhaps by a terrorist to hide his identity. Or, some would say it will legitimize same sex marriage. With an amended birth record in hand (changed from male to female), the new female would be free to enter into a legal marriage with a man.

It is important to for us to separate and exclude from the transgender discussion people with medical conditions who truly have a medical need for surgery and special consideration from the legal system. For example, a condition called intersex occurs where a person is born with ambiguous genitalia. This condition is extremely rare and those who have it are not considered transgenders. Sometimes individuals have abnormal patterns in their chromosomes. When medical tests objectively prove the need for surgery, revising the birth record could be necessary. Transgenders do not have a medical need for surgery. Desire does not equal need.

We as a society have now become enmeshed with the growing number of political sexual activists. When the truth is inconvenient, we exclude it. When facts get in the way, we make up our own, no matter how absurd or foolish. Often what remains has little resemblance to the truth. The absurdity of being asked to believe that a surgeon with a scalpel can change someone's gender is the greatest medical fraud in our lifetime. The transsexual has become the poster child for our changing social norms and social acceptance in the name of tolerance. But now, at least we know who the founders of the movement were and what their agenda was.

Dr. John Money was skilled at keeping the critics at bay. Dr. Money, at least for the first ten years, pushed back on the uncertainty and critics within Hopkins. Dr. Hoopes, a plastic surgeon and the first chairman of the Hopkins Gender Identity Clinic (GIC), gives us a view into how hard John Money advocated for patients for his gender surgery:

> *John Money would argue very forcefully that someone was a candidate ... that he knew the patient very well and **if this program was going to make any headway** this patient should be accepted (emphasis added).* [21]

This comment gives tremendous insight into Dr. Money's real agenda—the promotion and growth of the program, not necessarily good medical practice for patients. Money's desire to grow the program and promote gender change surgery was about making a name for himself as being the doctor who could redefine genders as we know it.

The media helped. They were salivating over stories that featured the new terms "transgender" and "sex change surgery." This was hot stuff, fresh and sexy, and far too titillating to be ignored by the media. People wanted to read about the twist of genders. The print media and television shows fell all over themselves featuring successful transgenders. What was hidden from public view was the dark side—30 to 50% of the transgender patients commit suicide, either before or in the years after the surgery. That's still true today, decades later.

Television talk shows on every major network feature gender altered men and women. No hard hitting print stories or television shows address the dark side of the surgical failures or deaths related to changing genders. Most of the television shows look like infomercials for changing genders. The positive stories keep the gender clinics active. Men requesting the removal of their unwanted appendages kept the surgeons, psychologists, electrolysis technicians, and plastic surgeons busy.

In 1969, Money conducted a follow-up study of seventeen male and seven female patients who had received surgery at the GIC. He reported, among other things, that after the operation, nine of the patients improved their occupational status and none declined. "All of the 17 [male-to-female patients] are unequivocally sure they have done for themselves the right thing," he wrote.[22] Dr. John Money's claims of success in the gender clinic made it easy to convince others to follow Hopkins "successful" lead. More clinics opened across America.

Dr. Money was agenda- and ego-driven, not integrity-driven. He was out to make a name for himself. Nothing defines better how wrong, twisted and corrupt Dr. John Money was than that one completely outrageous case of "gender change" on two-year-old David Reimer.

David was born in August, 1965. His circumcision (not done at Hopkins) was badly botched and the young boy's penis was accidently destroyed. The parents saw Dr. Money appear on television and contacted him for help about two years after the botched circumcision. John Money took this opportunity, without any medical justification whatsoever, to launch a medical experiment using David and his twin brother. Dr. Money recommended to the distraught parents that the best way to assure David's happiness was to surgically change his genitalia from male to female and raise him as a girl.

Dr. Money used the twins as an experiment to prove his theory that "gender was learned" and not innate at birth. He oversaw the case for many years and along the way he published articles about the success of reassigning a twin born a boy. Money acquired prestige and respect as an expert in sexual behavior and changing genders.

Sadly, it was not true. David never accepted that he was a girl, even though he was not told what had happened to him until age 14. He acted like a boy, through and through, to the dismay of his parents who were following Money's direction to reinforce David identity as female. David's gender change was a failure, in theory and in life.

Money knew through personal interaction with David that the

treatment had failed, yet he reported in scientific journals and his books that the child born a boy was happily living as a girl in every way—preferring girl activities and looking and acting feminine. By falsifying his results, Money misled the medical community and the public into thinking his experiment was successful. He got away with it because he kept David's identity a secret and no one was the wiser.

Money was so committed to showing how brilliant he was, for decades he was able to hide the real truth about the results of his studies on changing genders and the truth that he was a closet pedophile. If either were known, it would have greatly damaged his reputation.

Finally, in 2000, Money was exposed. David and his twin brother, then in their 30s, reluctantly went public. The twins told how Dr. Money had taken naked photos of both boys starting when they were seven years old, and how Dr. Money forced them to engage in incestuous sex with each other over the years. Clearly, Dr. Money inflicted pedophilic sexual abuse on the boys. The enormous pain of enduring sexual abuse, along with pouring out intimate details of their life to the media, and for David, the internal conflict from being raised a girl proved too much. Three years later, in 2003, David's brother was found dead, a drug overdose. David went to his brother's graveside four or five days a week; he was so distraught and in so much pain. David's wife was struggling to deal with David's depression and told him she wanted a separation. Soon after, David committed suicide at the age of 38.[23]

Dr. Reisman argues that Dr. John Money and his sex clinic at Johns Hopkins are directly complicit in both tragic deaths. With 30 years of lies, the nude photos, pedophilia and incestuous sexual abuse, no doubt Dr. John Money bears responsibility for both deaths. In his lifetime Dr. Money never flinched, always reporting in his patient documents and publicly that David's gender change had been a complete success. Even after David Reimer went public,

Dr. Money did not retract his findings or admit to the abusive nature of his sessions with the boys.

Let's go back to our story at the gender clinic at Johns Hopkins. In the mid 1970s, Dr. Paul McHugh became the Director of the Department of Psychiatry and Behavioral Sciences at the Johns Hopkins University School of Medicine, which included Money's gender identity clinic. Dr. McHugh took a fresh look at the gender clinic operating in his department. McHugh was not focused on advocating pedophilia or changing any social norms related to gender or homosexuality. McHugh was looking for the medical or psychological benefits from gender change surgery, some scientific evidence that Money's treatment with surgery was effective for patients with gender issues.

Now that the clinic had been treating patients for ten years, it was time to evaluate the success of the program. McHugh authorized Dr. Jon Meyer, the chairman of the Hopkins Gender Identity Clinic, to conduct a study in 1975. Dr. Meyer was not an outsider. As chairman of the clinic since 1969, he certainly was familiar with its workings and programs. It is likely they knew even prior to conducting the evaluation that the results would not be positive for continuing the surgeries.

Dr. Meyer chose as the subjects for the study fifty transsexuals who had been treated at Hopkins. The guidelines that the Hopkins Gender Identity Clinic imposed on wanna-be transsexuals were extremely stringent, so the study would include the most likely cases in the nation to show successful treatment by surgery. An article in *Baltimore Style* magazine describes Dr. Meyer's reaction to his results:

> *On Aug. 10, 1979, he [Dr. Jon Meyer] announced his results, which were far different than Money's a decade before. "To say that this type of surgery cures psychiatric disturbance is incorrect. We now have objective evidence*

that there is no real difference in the transsexual's adjustment to life in terms of jobs, educational attainment, marital adjustment and social stability," he said. [24]

Dr. Meyer discovered from the 50 interviews that those requesting the unusual gender surgery could be classified into two groups. The first group consisted of guilt-ridden homosexuals, men who saw the sex change as a way to resolve the conflict over same sex attraction. By living as a female, their attraction to men then looked normal but that did not always help. The second group consisted of mostly older men, heterosexual males (some bisexual) who found intense sexual arousal in cross-dressing as female. As they got older, they were eager to advance the costume of a female to a new level by undergoing a surgical transformation with breast implants and genital reconstruction, and therefore enhancing their arousal.

Both groups had all the same problems after surgery with work, relationships and emotions as they had prior to surgery. They did not improve psychologically; that remained the same. Both groups enjoyed cross-dressing prior to surgery and after surgery. No objective findings were noted. No noticeable improvement emerged in the 50 individuals as a result of Dr. Money's gender surgery procedure.[25]

Dr. Paul McHugh concluded:

We saw the results as demonstrating that just as these men enjoyed cross-dressing as women before the operation so they enjoyed cross-living after it. But they were no better in their psychological integration or any easier to live with. With these facts in hand I concluded that Hopkins was fundamentally cooperating with a mental illness. We psychiatrists, I thought, would do better to concentrate on trying to fix their minds and not their genitalia. [26]

Remarking in *The New York Times* on the results of the study,

Dr. Jon Meyer, who conducted the study, said:

> *My personal feeling is that surgery is not a proper treatment for a psychiatric disorder, and it's clear to me that these patients have severe psychological problems that don't go away following surgery.* [27]

The results of the study were completely contrary to Money's glowing reports of success and devastating to the program at Hopkins. But the damage had been done in terms of cementing in people's minds that sex change surgery was successful. Thanks to Dr. Money's fraud, gender surgery has been a big hit in America.

Dr. Stanley Biber

Led by the closure of the clinic at Johns Hopkins, university-affiliated gender clinics began to close across the country until only a few remained. Dr. Stanley Biber, a former Army MASH surgeon and friend of Dr. Money, had been performing the gender operation for 10 years at a hospital in Trinidad, Colorado. His first one, in 1969, occurred after a transsexual woman (a man) asked him if he would be willing and able to do so. Using diagrams from Hopkins, Dr. Biber figured out how to perform the surgery. His gender surgery practice grew and prospered in the dusty little town of Trinidad in the lower southeast corner of Colorado, especially after the university-affiliated gender clinics, his main competition, closed. Trinidad, Colorado, became known as the "sex change capital of the world." [28]

Dr. Stanley Biber continued to perform gender surgeries in Trinidad until his retirement in 2003 at age 79. Dr. Biber performed three to four gender surgeries a week and carved a permanent niche into history by performing more than 4,000 gender change surgeries in his lifetime. [29] That is a bunch of unwanted appendages.

Just to complete the picture, gender surgery didn't stop in

Trinidad with Dr. Biber's retirement. One of his former patients, Marci Bowers, a paper gender lady, moved into the Trinidad, Colorado gender change operating room when Biber retired. The media have elevated Bowers, the "transsexual surgeon," to superstar status, a free promotion for Bowers and her million-dollar-a-year surgery business. Prior to undergoing genital surgery at age 40, Bowers fathered three children. After the surgery, s/he remains legally married to his wife, yet engages in other relationships. The Kinsey dream of "anything goes" is alive.

Paul Walker

We have watched the passing of the gender surgery baton from Dr. Kinsey to Dr. Benjamin and then to Dr. Money, all of whom either supported or engaged in homosexuality and pedophilia. So, with the ink hardly dry on a report documenting the gender changing to be a failure as a treatment for gender issues, and the resultant closing of most university-based gender clinics across the country after 1979, who would be the successor to Dr. Money? Dr. John Money would pass the baton to none other than a friend and fellow psychologist, Dr. Paul Walker, a homosexual. Dr. Walker had spent time with Money at Hopkins as far back as the first transgender procedure in 1966. Dr. Walker was also friends with Harry Benjamin.

Benjamin and Money encouraged Walker to continue the national agenda and push to keep gender surgery alive despite the damaging report. So, Dr. Paul Walker took the next step—to form an association of gender surgery practitioners. In February 1979 in San Diego, at the Sixth International Gender Dysphoria Symposium, the formation of Harry Benjamin International Gender Dysphoria Association, using Benjamin's name by permission, was formally approved.

The people Dr. Walker selected for the founding committee fit a very familiar pattern: a pedophilia advocate, a homosexual, a sexual behaviorist and surgeons who benefit financially from performing the gender surgery:

Jack C. Berger, M.D., psychiatrist, University of Chicago

Richard Green, M.D., sexologist, and pedophilia advocate, graduate of Johns Hopkins medical school

Donald Laub, M.D., plastic surgeon, performing gender surgery, Mountain View, CA

Charles L. Reynolds, Jr., M.D., urologist

Leo Wollman, M.D., Ph.D, D.D., surgeon performing gender surgery, New York

The first order of business of the new association was the development of standards of care for gender identity disorders. Standards of care are guidelines, not requirements. Medical practitioners can choose to follow any or none of it. The founding committee, with Paul Walker as chairman, drafted the "The Standards of Care" in 1979. It has been revised several times over the years in an effort to resolve issues of patient regret and suicide. But the standards perhaps have been more effective at keeping the critics at bay.

It is safe to say the standards were used more like speed limit signs, almost never strictly adhered to. An unimpeachable source maintains that Dr. Walker himself, chairman of the committee that wrote the standards, was not inclined to follow them. The standards call for the psychologist to evaluate the candidate over the course of multiple sessions and for the candidate to live as the desired gender for a certain period of time before approval is given for the gender change. Dr. Walker provided an approval letter for a person in the summer of 1981 after one 45-minute office visit. No proper evaluation. No living as the intended gender. Poof! One session with Dr. Walker and off the patient went, approval letter in hand, to Dr. Biber for gender change surgery.

The standards of care, when first developed, were window

dressing, created and written to give the appearance of helping people and keeping them from making a rash decision for irreversible surgery. But the standards weren't followed then and are not followed today. It looks like the true purpose was (and is) to advance an agenda.

In an interview published in 1985, Benjamin urges caution and talks about the reality of regret:

> *One must understand the main problem of transsexuals. In English, it is properly named "gender dysphoria", i.e. a discrepancy between anatomy and sexual self-identification. It does not follow that one should perform surgery in every case, because there are cases in which such surgery is later regretted, sometimes many years later. Many transsexuals may also manage without surgery as long as they are being treated with hormones and can wear the clothing of the desired (more precisely: truly felt) sex. At the same time, some psychotherapy should be provided. As I said, this can occasionally be a tolerable solution. I myself am for the operation, but it should be applied critically and cautiously.[30]*

Benjamin's words, still true, are totally forgotten.

Fast-forward to today

Today approximately 20 surgeons around the country perform the surgery Dr. Money pioneered. The approval process is not intended to provide deep psychological evaluations that could uncover suicide ideation. In fact, laws are in place to restrict psychologists and the advice they may give to patients who wish to change genders. Imagine—the very professional that should be showing the patient the way to health is legally prohibited from saying anything that would discourage the patient from undergoing the irreversible surgery.

And who do you think lobbied the lawmakers for such restrictions in the first place? The gay, lesbian and transgender activists did. Why? Because many gender therapists are transsexuals themselves. It's a little like having the fox guarding the henhouse. Transsexual therapists have a vested interest to legitimize their own decision to undergo surgery by pushing others toward the same decision and silencing any voices of opposition.

What happens when the client has other issues that need addressing first, such as alcoholism, drug addiction or childhood abuse? Common sense says that changing genders will not solve those problems. The Hopkins study confirms it.

The prevailing tendency in the medical community is to allow patients to undergo all the surgery they want, rather than doing the tough work of deep evaluations. Gender changing has become the classic case of "if you want it, you can have it." Perhaps this propensity for surgery results in regret for those who change genders.

The gatekeepers for gender surgeries, according to the standards of care, are the psychologists. The process goes something like this: The transsexual wanna-be goes to the psychologist and requests approval for surgery. Any psychologist who wants to explore the patient's underlying issues, no matter how troubling, is barred legally from discouraging the patient, even if the psychologist feels the patient could be harmed by having surgery. On the other hand, any psychologist who is a gender activist will encourage the patient to take the path to switching genders. Either way, the patient receives overwhelming support for changing gender, with little or no diagnosis protocol followed.

The author personally knows of two recent cases where gender surgery was approved for young women, both of whom had been sexually abused by a family member. In one case, the patient's mother told the daughter's therapist about the abuse her daughter had endured. The therapist's response was, "If she wants switch genders, she can have surgery. She's 21." The therapist did not see the sexual abuse as an issue and approved the girl for surgery.

In the second case, the young girl not only had suffered sexual abuse outside the home by a family member, her mother was dying from cancer—a double whammy. The therapist did not see fit to address the profound issues and approved her for surgery.

Changing genders does not fix underlying issues. Imagine yourself in the shoes of someone who has suffered gender anxiety for years and all that time has dreamed about the happiness that will come with transition. Picture the enormous disappointment when happiness is short-lived and reality turns out differently.

An example played out in public view was the tragic case of Mike Penner, a popular and talented staff sports writer with a stellar 25-year career at *The Los Angeles Times*. No one will understand why Mike struggled and changed from identifying as Mike Penner, male, to being Christine Daniels, female. After he made the change to Christine in 2007, he continued to write his sports column under the byline Christine Daniels, and separately blogged about his gender change process. The response from his readers was overwhelmingly supportive. Because he was in a public profession, he became the "poster girl" for the transgender advocates. They used Christine all over the local television shows to promote the wonder of gender change. Unfortunately, even with overwhelming support, a great sports writer job and numerous transgender laws in place to protect gender changers, Mike did not stay in his new assigned gender. Without fanfare, he returned to using the Mike Penner byline in October 2008. A year later, he took his own life. As writer Kevin Spak says:

> *We'll never know if the Daniels identity was just a poor fit, or if external pressures drove the switch. The only thing we know is that life wasn't as easy for Christine Daniels*

or Mike Penner as they let on. It's a depressingly common problem—the suicide rate among transsexuals is 30-50%.[31]

The very existence of suicides in such large numbers is compelling testimony that changing genders is not an effective treatment, just as it was reported by the Johns Hopkins study thirty years prior.

The Smoking Gun

On one hand, we see reports of an extremely high rate of transgender suicide. On the other hand we see medical studies claiming that regret for the surgery is rare. The author receives emails from regretters regularly, so was not surprised by the suicide rate, but was puzzled by the glowing results reported by the medical community. Further analysis of the studies was made, looking for anything that could explain the discrepancy. Then what detectives call the "smoking gun" was discovered in a textbook called *Principles of Transgender Medicine and Surgery* (2007):

> *A large proportion of patients (up to 90%) are lost to follow up (emphasis added)... [which]...complicates efforts to systematically study the long-term effects of gender reassignment surgery.[32]*

The claim that regret is very rare is quite a leap, don't you think, when *up to 90%* of patients cannot be found. Indeed, any conclusions about success are pure speculation, not objective fact. It's easier to believe that the transgenders cannot be located because they committed suicide, are addicted to drugs, returned to their given name and birth gender or do not want to be found.

Giving transgenders false and misleading information has caused a deadly outcome for some. Perhaps we can start helping transgenders by telling them the truth: It is a paper change only. Scientifically it is impossible to change genders and no matter how many hormones you slam into your bloodstream you will remain forever in your birth gender.

Transgenders ask for tolerance of their gender change. Transgenders ask for political correctness, code for censuring any objections to their change. Then they ask us to play nice, by expanding diversity, code for adopting Kinsey's views on sexuality. Gender surgery was, and is, the means to a much larger social sexual agenda. The treatment goal for some gender changers is to fulfill sexual desires, perhaps giving us a clue as to why some commit suicide. Fulfilling sexual fantasies is a poor motivation for undergoing irreversible surgery and could easily lead to disappointment when the awful truth settles in.

Laura's Playground, a transgender support site that specializes in transgender suicide prevention, notes:

> *Every year thousands of Transgender lives are lost. Some of these are due to illegal hormone use, illegal procedures and liquid silicone injections that maim or kill. None of these though compare to the senseless and preventable loss of life due to Transgender suicide. Depending on who (sic) you talk to our suicide rate ranges anywhere from 31 to 50%.* **In a survey of Transsexuals here over 50% have had at least 1 suicide attempt by their 20th birthday.** *Some have been as young as 7 and many have had multiple attempts. If the **attempt rate** is that high imagine how many thousands have actually lost their lives in this year alone to suicide. Strangely the public and even the gay community are not outraged by these numbers. It is clear that if anything is to be done it needs to be shouldered by our own Transgender Community.*[33]

Suicide is the result of an unresolved psychiatric pathology. The deaths provide clear and sound evidence that switching genders is not a highly effective treatment. But the advocates knew that thirty years ago and pushed forward anyway even after most of the university-affiliated clinics closed. So bent on affecting change in our social and sexual norms, they refuse to look for alternative treatments that do not require hormones, surgery or changing birth records. Even with the "Standards of Care" in place, along with a plethora of new laws for employment, medical coverage and protection for transgenders, changing genders has not yet proven to be effective treatment.

Some activists for gender switching have advanced a theory that a *brain hormone wash* occurs in the womb during pregnancy and causes the desire to switch. This is a theory. But given the actual findings we have exposed, some others could argue persuasively the real brainwash is occurring every day on society by imposing terms like diversity (i.e., sexual), tolerance (even if the behavior is disgusting) and acceptance (of women who are not women).

Perhaps we can agree the gender change founders including Dr. Paul Walker, have not provided any sound evidence changing genders is a medical or psychological necessity. In fact, we now can see the recommended treatment, gender change, has a very high risk of suicide. We can also see the lack of objective medical findings for people like Mike Penner and others who truly needed our very best medical practitioners providing sound treatments. It's just not there. The result is lost lives.

Chapter 2.

Transgender Children

In 2005, Dr. Norman Spack shocked many across the country when he started injecting hormone blockers into the blood streams of young boys seven to twelve years old—a treatment he says is for gender identity disorder. Dr. Spack, a board-certified pediatrician and pediatric endocrinologist and Associate Professor of Pediatrics at Harvard Medical School, has started a gender clinic for children at prestigious Children's Hospital Boston, the primary pediatric teaching hospital of Harvard Medical School. But this time the media is not so quick to give genius status; the skeptics line up.

Dr. Spack uses a special drug therapy modeled after Dutch researchers to delay the onset of puberty.[34] The hormone blockers are powerful. Hormone blockers do not change DNA birth gender, but keep the body from undergoing the physical changes of puberty that make a person appear male or female. The hormone blocking therapy is the first step to changing genders for young people, followed by cross-gender hormone therapy and finally, gender change surgery.

Dr. Spack's contention (theory) is that treating children with gender change before the onset of puberty will result in greater satisfaction. For example, men who transition to women in adulthood have a hard time fitting in ("passing") as women because puberty causes them to appear masculine in irreversible ways—harder jaw line, bigger hands, taller, bigger boned, facial hair. Spack says treat the patients at a younger age, prior to puberty's changes. The results, good or bad, on the lives of the children that Dr. Spack has treated with hormone blockers or cross-gender hormone therapy are yet to be published or scrutinized by his peers. His treatments are experimental, and he is experimenting on children.

Even though Dr. Spack works very closely with children, he has not kept a distance from homosexual pedophiles. In 2006, Dr. Spack presented a workshop at a Transcending Boundaries conference co-sponsored by *The New England Leather Alliance (NELA)*.[34-2] NELA, according to its Facebook entry, is an "organization dedicated to the support, education, and political organizing of the leather /fetish / SM [sado-masochism]/ bondage communities in New England." Dr. Spack's sexual proclivities are unknown, but his documented connection to bondage and sado-masochism is very troubling. Frankly speaking, the connection of a pediatrician to pedophilia *in any way* should raise more than an eyebrow or two.

Almost 50 years after Dr. John Money, a pedophile advocate, used the prestigious Johns Hopkins gender clinic to promote gender surgery for adults, we have a similar pattern. It is difficult to ignore that doctors who advocate for the transgender surgeries somehow are aligned with pedophilia, as we discovered with Drs. Alfred Kinsey, Harry Benjamin and John Money. This consistent pedophile connection strongly suggests that the doctors themselves suffer from an unresolved obsessive mental illness.

Dr. Spack, like Dr. Money before him, is so focused on the advancement of changing genders he never considers if it is effective treatment. During the last 35 years numerous studies have been made around the world stating that there is no objective evidence showing that changing genders is an effective treatment for gender disorders. Dr. Spack has said much more research still needs to be done regarding how transgenderism occurs.[35] It took years for the Hopkins Gender Clinic of the 1970s to learn the treatment failed to help the patient. Perhaps it will be only after years of botching children's lives that the practice will change.

Why, now, is it okay to experiment on young kids? Maybe it has a lot to do with the cumulative effects on our society of many influences. Kinsey's "sexual revolution" devalued children and portrayed them as sex objects. The routine practice of abortion as just one more method of birth control promotes the view that it's okay to kill an unborn child simply for the convenience of the parents. Homosexual and transgender activists have become increasingly successful in getting laws passed that further their agenda. When combined, the effects on how we as a society perceive children are staggering, providing a backdrop for experimenting on children.

Society/cultural backdrop

Parents with young school-aged children today face difficult challenges because of the many outside influences and agendas aimed squarely at indoctrinating youth. In 1948 Kinsey threw his own bedroom door open and claimed his perverted ways represented normal Americans, thus changing our social norms for the worse. Now Kinsey's long-reaching legacy has entered the schoolyard. Advocacy and acceptance of homosexuality, pedophilia and transsexualism are slowly but surely being included in school curriculum.

One such example in California is Senate Bill 777, passed in 2007. Thanks to SB 777, written by and advanced by a lesbian who has no kids in school, the public schools are now ground zero for advocating homosexuality and gender change. The homosexual, lesbian and transgender extremists quietly won a major assault on children's minds.

SB 777 requires schools to not just teach reading, writing and arithmetic, but mandates that when schoolchildren as young as kindergarten participate in school-sponsored activities, those activities must positively portray cross-dressing, sex change, and *all* aspects of homosexuality.[36] The word *all* includes pedophilia.

Health Advisor to President Obama

One of President Obama's top health care advisors is Dr. Peter Singer, a Princeton University philosophy professor. Dr. Singer advocates killing babies up to one month old if they have Down syndrome or similar disabilities. In his own words: "A period of 28 days after birth might be allowed before an infant is accepted as having the same right to life as others."[37]

At the Governor's Commission on Disability in Concord, N.H., on October 5, 2001, according to the Associated Press, Peter Singer made the comment:

> *"I do think that it is sometimes appropriate to kill a human infant," he said, adding that he does not believe a newborn has a right to life until it reaches some minimum level of consciousness.*[38]

Dr. Singer believes that killing disabled babies is ethically sound behavior. As medical advisor to President Obama, he has much influence on the content and application of "ObamaCare" legislation. What a way to save money on medical care—kill disabled babies. Forget the debate on abortion. Just wait until they are born, then kill them. Are you beginning to think that the real nuts in our society are the advocates who are also doctors? Even worse, the president of our nation, Barack Obama, thinks this man Singer has the credibility to advise his administration on the ethical issues of health care.

Obama's Safe Schools Czar

One of the advocates' goals seems to be the breakdown of the taboo against adults having sex with children. The advocates call such abhorrent behavior "consensual" instead of what it really is: predatory child abuse. They suggest and provide materials that are sexually explicit to public schools under the guise of "recommended reading lists."[39]

In 2009, President Obama appointed Kevin Jennings, founder and long-time director of the Gay, Lesbian and Straight Education Network (GLSEN), as Safe Schools Czar. Kevin Jennings advocates adult sex with children, just like Kinsey did. Instead of protecting young boys from being used by adults for criminal sex acts, Mr. Jennings says to the child: "Use a condom." [40] Under Jennings' direction, his organization, GLSEN, published a recommended reading list for middle school and high school students supposedly meant to promote tolerance and understanding of gays, but it included many sexually-graphic books of adults having sex with children,[41] implying that this, too, should be tolerated and accepted.

The controversy surrounding his appointment is related in an editorial by Angela Wilson on examiner.com:

> Shortly after his appointment as Safe Schools Czar, controversy erupted regarding an incident that occurred while Jennings was a high school teacher. In his 1994 book, "One Teacher in Ten: Gay and Lesbian Educators Tell Their Stories," Jennings describes his conversation with a 15 or 16 year old student, "Brewster." Brewster told Jennings about an encounter he had with a man he met in a bus station restroom, and that he subsequently went home with the man. Jennings' response to the story was to tell Brewster to be sure to wear a condom.

Critics believe that the appropriate response of a teacher upon hearing this story should have been (at minimum) to highlight the dangers of having sex with a stranger and to try to discourage future encounters of this sort. [42]

The Washington Times in an editorial about the appointment of Jennings said:

> *The evidence suggesting he [Kevin Jennings] is unfit to serve as a senior presidential appointee is startling and plentiful. It was revealed this week that Mr. Jennings was involved in promoting a reading list for children 13 years old or older that made the most explicit sex between children and adults seem normal and acceptable. This brought up anew Mr. Jennings' past controversies, such as his seeming encouragement of sex between one of his high school students and a much older man as well as his praise for Harry Hay, a notorious supporter of the North American Man Boy Love Association.[43]*

Medicine and Science

Taken together, the effects of these various influences provide an environment where experimentation on children is seen as acceptable.

Dr. Spack and the Children's Hospital Boston, by treating children who have obvious gender difficulties with experimental long-lasting treatments, could be playing Russian roulette with children's lives. Long-term studies have yet to be published that validate whether his treatment regimen of puberty blockers and cross-gender hormones is appropriate; at this time, he's just testing a theory. Suicides and other ill effects may come long after the treatment. We can remember the Reimer twins as an example: well into adulthood, one committed suicide and the other died from a drug overdose.

Is it wise to let a doctor give children strong puberty blocking drugs? Some will consider this treatment child abuse and it could well be. Dr. Spack says that the effects of puberty blockers are totally reversible. Does that make it safe?

That promise sounds good to the parents and to the public but it ignores the reality—people who are driven to change their gender don't stop with the blockers. They can easily obtain hormones, those powerful body-changing hormones, with or without a prescription or a doctor. It's foolish to believe otherwise.

Hormones cause the body to develop in certain ways and some effects are irreversible, such as bone size and height. What will the doctors do for the boy who discovers he made the wrong choice and wants to go back and be male? He realizes that his psyche was not cured with surgery or by his new looks. He now looks like a girl. How can this not have long-term effects?

I would like to see the use of hormone blockers replaced with an explanation to the child the same way Washington, D.C., pediatrician Ivor Horn counsels her patients' parents: "It's important to let children know they're okay the way they are, that you love them that way, that the changes in their body are normal, and they can come to you with any questions."[44] Help the children to understand that these changes occur naturally during this time of childhood and not to stop the process with hormone blockers as if puberty were a mistake.

The truth is: it is impossible to actually change someone's gender. Why, then, start the child off on a life filled with lies? When doctors and parents cannot bring themselves to tell the truth, the child's world becomes one of imagination, fantasy and elaborate masquerades, none of which is emotionally healthy for the child.

Could the Diagnosis Be Wrong?

Dr. Spack says he took his lead for this radical therapy from the

Dutch so let's see just what the Dutch think. With a little digging, an article was located called *Psychiatric Comorbidity of Gender Identity Disorders: a Survey among Dutch Psychiatrists*, published in the American Journal of Psychiatry in July 2003.[45] Comorbidity simply means that more than one condition is occurring in an individual. Practically speaking, the patient is suffering from more than one malady.

The objective of the study was to explore the extent to which gender identity disorder can be distinguished from other disorders that may be present. The motivation for the study was the liberalization of treatment guidelines in the Netherlands that allows hormonal and surgical sex reassignment therapy to be started at puberty or pre-puberty.[46] This treatment causes irreversible effects, so it becomes incredibly important to make the correct diagnosis, especially on youngsters.

In the U.S., the tendency is to treat everyone who presents with the "I'm in the wrong body" symptom with a one-size-fits-all type of treatment, changing the body to fit the psychosis. It seems too simplistic. What if the person suffers from some other disorder and this happens to be the symptom? Are there any other illnesses that should be ruled out before undertaking irreversible surgeries?

For example, the same Dutch comorbidity study says that 25% of those who suffer from schizophrenia exhibit cross-gender desires.[47] But schizophrenia typically cannot be definitively diagnosed until the early 20s. So treating a teenager or pre-teen with a gender change protocol which irreversibly alters their bodies "just in case" they have gender identity disorder will result in mistreating those who, instead, are schizophrenic.

In a nutshell, the Dutch physicians who responded to the survey reported that in 61% of the cases, patients were also diagnosed with other psychiatric disorders. And in three-fourths of these patients, the patient's desire to become the opposite gender was associated *not* with gender identity disorder, but was the symptom of other psychiatric illnesses, notably personality, mood, dissociative, and psychotic disorders.[48] The fact that psychotic disorders are often mentioned as co-existing with gender identity disorder calls for a very careful evaluation of the benefits and risks when considering cross gender treatments.

Based on this Dutch survey, if physicians had treated all the patients with hormone treatment and gender changing surgery, they would have missed the actual cause of the behavior in almost *half* of the patients while causing irreversible changes in their lives.

Comorbidity with psychiatric illnesses is only one part of the misdiagnosis puzzle. Another cause of the desire to become the other gender lies in the endocrine, or hormone, system of the body. For some men, as the male hormone testosterone level rises naturally during puberty, they experience an overwhelming desire to dress as women or to become women. Dr. Anne Vitale, Ph.D., a therapist who counsels transgenders in San Rafael, California, writes:

> *I became suspicious of testosterone being the hormone that causes gender dysphoria in some genetic males. Obviously this is not true for the vast majority of males; they do just fine on normal levels of testosterone (300-999 ng/dl). However, a subset of genetic males appear to respond to testosterone in a manor[sic] that evokes an overwhelming desire to express feelings of femininity.[49]*

In the one-size-fits-all model of treatment in the U.S. today, this diagnosis is likely to be missed because no one is looking for it. The man with an "overwhelming desire" will be encouraged to continue with hormone treatment and gender changing surgery. The author knows an individual who underwent the surgery and discovered by accident over 25 years later that his testosterone, although well within the normal range for a man, was causing the overwhelming desire to switch genders. He just needed to adjust his male hormone levels for the feeling to subside. He now lives fully as a male, hormones adjusted. You could call him a "boomerang transgender" because he underwent surgery to appear female, and later went back to his original male gender. He is probably not the only man to experience this anomaly.

The surgery-happy doctors are much too quick to push for irreversible surgery, going for the knife first. A wide range of potential issues could be causing the symptoms, yet the alternates are not explored. Even when the transgender therapists have such information, they are reluctant to advise a course of treatment that does not have surgical intervention as its end goal.

Hormones are powerful. Many transgenders buy hormones directly over the internet without the benefit of blood tests or seeing a doctor who can assess possible hormone imbalances. They could be aggravating their symptoms, rather than helping.

Isn't the Surgery Medically Necessary?

When you see the term "medically necessary" used to describe gender change treatment understand this—the idea evolves from statements found in the Harry Benjamin Standards of Care written by homosexual activists to advance their agenda. The activists have successfully duped most everyone into thinking that sex change surgery is medically necessary, even though the surgery is cosmetic only. It is the opinion of the author that the primary reason they are so insistent on that specific terminology is to force insurance companies or the government to pay the cost—$25,000 to $70,000 per patient. The only medically necessary part of the sex surgery is the patient's desire to have someone else pay for it.

Some examples may help. Medically necessary is amputating a limb because of gangrene infection. Medically necessary is providing prescription medication for depression in concert with good and constant long-term psychotherapy. *Not* medically necessary is removing perfectly good body parts or giving some guy breast implants so he can cosmetically look different.

Every once in awhile, someone sees through the transgender smoke screen, like one member of the Canadian Parliament, Pierre Poilievre, who said regarding reinstating coverage of sex surgery costs by the Ontario health care system:

> *"We need to ensure that every single dollar goes to medically necessary treatments, and prevent Ontario from funding sex reassignment surgery."*[50]

I have no doubt some people want the surgery badly and would in fact enjoy acting out in a different gender role, but medically necessary? No. More on this in a later chapter.

Is the Child Capable of Making this Decision?

Dr. Spack says he doesn't believe lifelong decisions should be made at ages 10-12 for girls and ages 12-14 for boys. He says they should wait until age 16, when they are old enough to understand the long-term consequences of proceeding with gender change.

But the research says that is still too young. Researchers across the country have collaborated in a large project to map the development of the brain from childhood through adulthood. What they have found is that the very areas in the brain that provide the ability to plan for the future and foresee consequences do not mature until the early 20s.[51]

Says Dr. Jay Giedd of the National Institute of Mental Health: "Teens are capable of enormous intellectual and artistic accomplishments. But that basic part of the brain that gives us strategies and organizing and perhaps warns us of potential consequences isn't fully on board yet."[52]

Dr. Andrew Garner of the American Academy of Pediatrics notes that the adolescent brain is still developing through the teen years and not yet fully mature until age 24.[53]

So Dr. Spack's idea that a child of age five or seven, ten or twelve, or even sixteen can make decisions about gender treatments that carry lifelong consequences appears to be misguided. Just think about it. Spack feels kids have the maturity to know how they will respond years later to making a gender change but research shows that the brain is not mature enough to understand. Psychologists with educated mature brains struggle to understand the implications of gender issues and their treatment, how then can we expect a teenager to comprehend them?

Gender: Formed in the womb or through experience?

What has been suggested by the transgender activists is that kids are born transgender because the hard wiring of the brain occurs in the womb. Dr. Spack also says gender identity is formed at birth and is not a product of the environment.[54]

That's a theory, but is it true? We know that gender found in the DNA is established in the womb. But how a child acts out their gender role can vary and depends on the parents, siblings and anyone else who spends time with the child.[55]

Babies are born as fully equipped, batteries-included, ready-to-go, learning machines, prepared to explore and equipped to be stimulated by the world around them. Researchers have confirmed that the way parents interact with their child in the early years and the experiences they provide help shape the developing structures of the brain. As the brain matures and grows, the baby learns various functions like seeing, hearing, moving, and expression of emotion. What the baby sees and hears shapes their views of the world and that can be good or bad.[56]

Researchers are looking into the role of early experiences on gender. Susan Witt, Ph.D., Professor of Child Development at the University of Akron, writes:

> As children move through childhood and into adolescence, they are exposed to many factors which influence their attitudes and behaviors regarding gender roles. These attitudes and behaviors are generally learned first in the home and are then reinforced by the child's peers, school experience, and television viewing. However, the strongest influence on gender role development seems to occur within the family setting, with parents passing on, both overtly and covertly, to their children their own beliefs about gender.[57]

Far too much advocating for gender switching goes on. The many other psychological, hormonal and childhood potential causes for the patient's distress are rarely, if ever, explored first in an effort to prevent the surgery. The result is misdiagnosis, mistreatment, and lives irrevocably altered.

Real Life Stories

The author has received many emails from men who have completed the transition from male to female. You can see in their own words some of the pitfalls they have encountered.

This first email is from a male-to-female (MTF) transgender who recently had the surgery. The man had the full surgery and now is returning to his birth gender. No group is more scorned and unprotected by laws than those who discover the surgery treatment to be a fraud and wish to undo it. They are bullied by the homosexuals and other transsexuals.

Sent: April 11, 2009

I recently had the sex change surgery, and although I thought I was completely sure of what I was doing, I began to regret the decision a mere three weeks after the operation. Some might say I was experiencing post-op depression, but it was definitely more than that. I also suspect that many of the other patients at the hospital who had the same operation experienced similar feelings based on my discussions with them. What really drove the point home for me was the realization that it required eight hours on an operating table to make my genitalia appear to be female. That pretty much tells me that I'm NOT female at all. If I were female, why wasn't I born with female genitalia? Sure, there are some intersexed people with ambiguous genitals, but I'm not at all intersexed. My chromosomes are the normal male XY, with absolutely no abnormalities.

The reality is that I'm male, and no amount of surgery changes that fact. I'm now four months post-op, and I've begun to transition to live as a male again. I feel it's the only way to be honest with myself and with society. If you are considering this surgery, think very carefully about the consequences. Make sure that the doctor or counselor that's approving you for the surgery is qualified to evaluate whether you need the operation or not. So many unnecessary operations of this type are carried out each year around the world, and in all too many cases, the effect is pain and regret not only for the person who had the operation, but also for their families.

From another MTF transgender, ten years after the surgery:

I underwent surgery about 10 years ago. I was convinced it was the right thing to do - regrettably, it was not. The price I paid was dear; I hurt the ones I loved the most—my children, my siblings, my parents, and my partner.

By all appearances I am a success story. I have a good job as a high school teacher, I live stealth, have had a fairly active love life, etc., but none of this can ever make up for the pain and guilt I feel everyday of my life. As accepting as my son has been, every time I look at him I see the hurt in his eyes. I can feel his sense of loss over his father, and it tears at my very soul.

Believe it or not, I have even gone to a therapist and several surgeons—with little success. I just get told it's a normal part of the "adjustment phase" (an awfully long phase!!!). They say, "You make a nice woman—be happy!" But I'm not happy!

I am wondering if you know of any surgeon that will remove my breast implants. I really would like to start living as a man again.

Two letters. The first demonstrates the case where regret comes very quickly, just three weeks after surgery. The second letter shows someone who, even after 10 years as a "success" story, wants to return to his birth gender. If changing genders is so good, why do they want to return to their birth gender? Perhaps because the birth gender is real and the paper gender doesn't live up to expectations.

The following emails from other transgenders and their parents demonstrate what some of the family relationships looked like during their childhoods. The names have been removed to protect the identity of the people. You decide—in each of these cases is hard wiring of gender determined in the womb or during early childhood?

From a transgender son—notice how he describes his parents:

Sent: Fri, November 19, 2010 11:41:23 AM
Subject: Re: Personal Question

My parents are both alcoholics and my mum has recently died. They abused us as children. I have 2 brothers 1 older and 1 younger. They are cool about my transgender now that my mum has died and my dad too accepts the fact I want to be a woman please.

I am 26 and I have been taking hormones for the last 18 months. Just after Christmas I will have the operation. I am bisexual because I like the best of both worlds and enjoy lots of sex. You could say I'm a sexaholic.

The next email is from the mother of a transgender. In an earlier email, she described the family environment. She's been married three times. Her first husband, the father of her son, was an abusive alcoholic, and home life was chaotic. No blame has been attached to anyone here; this is just the reality of home life. We get to see that the consequence in some cases is the onset of a desire in the child to live a transgender life.

Sent: Fri, November 26, 2010 7:48:12 PM

I was surprised to learn that my son had been approved to begin sex reassignment treatment already. I didn't consider it unusual that he as the oldest would take that role he had always wanted to be the "mom" in a play activity. That did not continue beyond the age of 8 or 9. Or so I thought. I learned later and what I didn't know, but became aware of almost two years ago, was that as a part of the pagan involvement, my son engaged in orgies and bi-sexuality. It was through his then-fiancée/now wife's blog that I learned of these things. He told me he intends to continue with the hormones to make an outward physical transformation.

He and his wife are actively involved in GLTB [gay-lesbian-trans-bisexual] advocacy groups and have served as panel participants at conference events. It is as though they are enjoying the celebrity of his gender switch. His experiences in cross dressing and gender identification have coincided with her studies and she has used them as topics in her coursework. Knowing these things makes it difficult not to believe that undue emphasis has been placed on gender issues in my son's life experiences. His wife is also a transgender, female to male.

The next note is from a mother torn apart by her son's (MTF) actions:

Sent: Tue, August 10, 2010 9:43:15 AM
Subject: My Transgender Son

You graciously replied to my email after I read your first book about a year ago. That is the month my son went to Mexico and had 11 more surgeries in one day. He is now 24 and has had almost 30 surgeries. He asked if I would go to Thailand for his sex reassignment, my answer was no. All of this has affected me much. I no longer have any contact with him. His dad does and that's all I need to know. My son is very angry and has done some name calling, and told the lie that I abandoned him.

During a subsequent meeting with her and her husband, it was learned that they had used drugs during their son's early childhood. Parents with substance addictions tend to be emotionally unavailable, so it's highly likely that their son's accusation of abandonment has a sound basis. Both parents are good people and painfully aware that they took some wrong turns. Sadly, the consequences are difficult to absorb or repair.

Suicide: Lethal consequence

The question is: Why don't the activists take action to stop the transgender suicides among teens? But remember the activists' motto is: "Never let a crisis go to waste." News stories regularly appear about bullying in schools directed against homosexuals and transgenders, and the activists claim that the bullying is causing suicide. "We need more laws!" is their rallying cry. The activists are using the suicides to push for more legislation to benefit their group.

Let's uncouple a few things here. Bullying needs to be addressed, of course. But there is no proof that schoolyard bullying accounts for the high rate of suicide among transgenders, young or old. In the quest to promote laws, the activists fail to lobby the medical community to investigate the reasons behind the suicides. Improvements to the diagnostic process could help prevent the suicides of so many transgenders. Doctors should consider treatments that do not require changing genders and look at suicide prevention models.

At least 90 percent of people who kill themselves have a diagnosable and treatable psychiatric illnesses—such as major depression, bipolar depression, or some other depressive illness, including schizophrenia, alcohol or drug abuse, posttraumatic stress disorder or other anxiety disorder, bulimia or anorexia nervosa, or personality disorders.[58] Depression itself has many causes, such as being the victim of domestic violence, rape, assault, or physical, verbal or sexual abuse.

It is very rare that someone dies by suicide because of one cause. Usually several causes, not just one, will drive someone to commit suicide. Most people die by suicide when several negative life experiences occur, and the person does not receive proper treatment, or does not receive effective treatment. Some people need to go through several different treatments until they find one that works for them.

So if a transgender male moves all the way through the transition process—avoiding suicide, not faltering on the journey and completes the cosmetic surgeries—what is next? He gets a new birth record and gets all other supporting documents changed, and lives as a woman. Is the outcome one of "happy ever after"?

We know some percentage will commit suicide in the process. Suicide rates are not easy to nail down because the samples change with each study, but here is what we do know for sure. Transgenders often have depression and psychological issues that go untreated.

On top of that they abuse illicit drugs and alcohol to a greater degree than the general population and as a result have more medical problems. The transition from one gender to another is very difficult emotionally, physically, and socially. This makes for a dangerous cocktail that can result in suicide.

In a national survey of 7,000 transgenders who were asked "Have you ever attempted suicide?" 41% answered yes.[59] "I knew that the magnitude would be high, but I did not think the suicide attempt numbers would be that high," said clinical psychologist Gail Knudson, a professor in the department of sexual medicine at the University of British Columbia and medical director of the Transgender Health Program at Vancouver Coastal Health Knudson. The percentage is corroborated by another source that says among transgender people ages 18-44, the suicide attempt rate was 45%.[60]

The U.S. medical community and media would have you believe that gender changing surgery is the only successful treatment for gender identity disorder. However, the high rate of suicide attempts by transgender adolescents could suggest that, for a significant portion of those treated for gender identity issues, the primary psychological issue is being misdiagnosed and untreated.

As of now, *60 Minutes*, *Nightline* or some other investigative show has failed to produce stories such as those seen in the letters presented here. The author has been contacted three or four times to be part of a segment show, but when he explained he wanted to talk about the regret and suicide, they were less enthusiastic.

The testimonies, research findings and the suicide attempt rate indicate that gender changing surgery has not yielded great results for everyone. So why do the experiments continue on kids? Why does a children's gender clinic have as its director a doctor who is aligned with activist groups that support pedophilia? This has become an all too familiar pattern.

Summary

The take away from this chapter is learning the unspeakable, that young kids have become the tools of the trade for the advancement of the activist homosexual agenda.

Transgenders are not born that way, but made out of early childhood impressions. Young kids should not be subjected to any medical hormone intervention until their late teens or early 20s, if it is required. Dr. Spack and others play a reckless game of unknown consequences with kids who are used as experiments without providing treatment for the more serious psychological issues that could be causing the youngsters to exhibit gender identity confusion.

Coming Up

For a long time, a conflict of opinion has existed between surgeons and psychotherapists over how to treat psychological disorders. Some surgeons have attempted to render psychotherapy irrelevant by advancing surgery as the treatment of choice for psychological disorders. The result is a hundred years of a dark and shameful history of "medically necessary" surgeries that were not really medically necessary at all.

As you will see in the next chapters, doctors have a long history of forging ahead with unproven medical surgeries, often with very tragic results. Some doctors so enjoy being in the limelight, that they close their eyes to the serious risks their treatments pose to their patients. You will become acquainted with some infamous examples of the lengths to which doctors will go to ignore, hide, and muzzle the truth about their failed surgical procedures.

Chapter 3.

The Ice Pick Doctor

To catch a glimpse of the long-term clinical success we might expect from gender surgery, let's take a look at some of the history of psychosurgery. The term psychosurgery means intervening surgically in order to treat mental illness, such as depression and other psychological issues.

In the last 100 years some radical psychosurgical interventions which gained prominence followed a certain cycle. First we see great optimism, accompanied by glowing media reports on the success and promise of the new treatment. That fuels demand for the procedure from the public. Along the way, some suspicion rises from others in the medical community that it can't be the miracle cure the practitioners are claiming it to be. At last, after decades of practice and thousands of patients later, the results on real patients are objectively analyzed and we learn the sorry truth: No help for a significant percentage of patients, and in the wake of the treatment, a trail of broken lives and families.

Lobotomy was the miracle intervention of the 1930s and 40s. It was advanced by a fame-hungry doctor and embraced by mental institutions as a means to alleviate their overcrowding. The state saw it as a way to lower the costs of providing for the mentally ill. Throw in a media willing to sing its praises, a community of depressed patients without any hope and you have everything necessary for the medical equivalent of a train wreck.

Watch as we unfold the story of lobotomy for the striking parallels to gender surgery—the unproven results, the irreversible nature of the surgery, and the media's part in influencing public acceptance of the treatment.

The story of the lobotomy in the U.S. starts at a meeting of the Southern Medical Society in Baltimore in 1936. Neurologist Dr. Walter Freeman and his surgeon associate Dr. James Watts announced the results of their first six cases of the use of lobotomy, surgery that severs connections in the brain. They reported that anxiety, confusion, phobias, hallucinations, and delusions had been relieved or erased entirely in some patients.[61] A reporter from the *Baltimore Sun* who was there that day reported that Freeman's presentation was received with "sharp criticism and cries of alarm… one man after another…joined in the chorus of the hostile cross-examiners."[62] Into the fray stepped Dr. Adolph Meyer, a prominent professor at Johns Hopkins University since the early 1900s and proponent of psychosurgery. Meyer forcefully changed the tone and ended the sharp criticism of Freeman. "I am not antagonist to this work," he informed the attendees, "but I find it very interesting. The available facts are sufficient to justify the procedure in the hands of responsible persons." Meyer won the day. Drs. Freeman and Watts' practice of lobotomy had cleared its first hurdle, thanks to timely support from the influential Meyer.

Some called it barbaric, the frontal lobotomy procedure adapted by Freeman and Watts and originally pioneered by neurologist Egas Moniz (1874–1955) of Portugal. People must have been impressed by it. Moniz was awarded a Nobel Prize for medicine in 1949. Lobotomies were not proven medically necessary but rather were experimental and performed on many who later, it was found, did not need the radical procedure at all. The Nobel Prize was awarded to Moniz? What were they thinking? Maybe the attraction to the procedure may have been because it was so outrageous.

Dr. Walter Jackson Freeman II (1895–1972) was a neurologist and psychiatrist. He graduated from Yale and the University of Pennsylvania Medical School. He was president of the American Association of Neuropathology from 1944 to 1945 and president of the American Board of Psychiatry and Neurology from 1946 to 1947.[63]

Dr. Freeman was not a surgeon and had no surgical training. He teamed with his colleague, surgeon Dr. James Watts, in order to perform prefrontal lobotomy. The procedure required entering through the skull in an operating room and cutting the fibers that connected different parts of the brain.[64]

Dr. Walter Freeman, always the showman, became so well known that he was sought out by Joe Kennedy, the future President John F. Kennedy's father, to help his 23 year old daughter, Rosemary. Rosemary was Joe and Rose Kennedy's third child, their first daughter, born in September, 1918. Laurence Leamer in his book, *The Kennedy Women*, describes her as "painfully slow…a pretty child with green eyes that peered out on life directly."[65]

Rosemary was just not the daughter Joe felt he could be proud of. Kennedy thought she was too moody and depressed and a possible risk of embarrassment to him and the Kennedy family. She could be aggressive and angry and the family feared that she was going out into the streets to do what her sister Kathleen called "the thing the priest says not to do."

Joe Kennedy began consulting with a physician from George Washington University named Walter Freeman, who was experimenting with a new form of brain surgery called lobotomy. Dr. Freeman sold Joe Kennedy a bill of goods. He said that the biggest drawback of the procedure for a female patient was the fact that her head would have to be shaved and she would not want to be seen in public until her hair grew back.

Only five years after Dr. Freeman first initiated the use of his new lobotomy procedure to treat mental illness, in 1941, the wealthy Kennedy patriarch turned over his 23 year old daughter for the radical procedure.

What Joe may have wanted all along was "no worries" about Rosemary. The former ambassador did not want to run the risk that she could embarrass him. He was powerful, unstoppable, heavy-handed and unyielding.

Rosemary was wheeled into the operating room. Freeman's associate drilled a hole in her skull and inserted a sort of spatula into her brain and began digging. Freeman asked her to sing simple songs and perform basic addition and subtraction. As long as she could recite the doggerel, and handle third-grade arithmetic, they kept digging. Finally, though, Rosemary Kennedy fell silent, and the operation was over. And for all practical purposes, so was Rosemary's life.

Prior to surgery, Rosemary was able to do arithmetic and write in her diary. After the surgery, she was rendered infantile and incontinent. Her verbal skills were reduced to unintelligible babble. She went from being "slow" to being institutionalized. She would never recover. If being a bit slow or sometimes aggressive in our early adulthood were reason for receiving a frontal lobotomy, we would all be in trouble.

"The procedure had regressed her into an infant like state," author Laurence Leamer writes, "mumbling a few words, sitting for hours staring at the walls, only traces left of the young woman she had been, still with flashes of rage. This was a horror beyond horror, an unthinkable, unspeakable disaster. Rose and her children had repressed so much, and now they repressed what Joe had done to his daughter, repressed it all and pretended that it had never happened and that Rosemary no longer existed."[66]

Joe Kennedy's decision for surgery was brutally callous and

horrific. The media, perhaps at his instruction, buried the story and Rosemary along with it, not exposing Dr. Freeman for what he was, a real quack.

In the late 1970s, Bobby Kennedy's son, David, was reading a copy of the pro-drug magazine *High Times* when he came across a story on lobotomies. Naturally enough, one of the illustrations was a photo of his beautiful aunt Rosemary, pre-lobotomy.

"She had a new pair of white shoes on," David recalled later for the authors Peter Collier and David Horowitz of *The Kennedys: An American Drama.* "The thought crossed my mind that if my grandfather was alive the same thing could have happened to me that happened to her. She was an embarrassment; I am an embarrassment. She was a hindrance; I am a hindrance. As I looked at this picture, I began to hate my grandfather and all of them for having done the thing they had done to her and for doing the thing they were doing to me."[67]

Rosemary Kennedy was not an isolated case. The sister of noted American playwright Tennessee Williams had several nervous breakdowns and was diagnosed as a schizophrenic. After many unsuccessful attempts at therapy, she was finally subjected to a prefrontal lobotomy in 1943, in Washington D.C.[68] As in the case of Rosemary Kennedy, the surgery was botched, and she was disabled for life. This was a great shock for Tennessee Williams, who was very attached to his sister, and the failed lobotomy probably became a factor in driving Williams to alcoholism.[69]

Even with the dismal results on Rosemary and many other patients, Freeman continued and became extremely financially successful. He and his lobotomy teams performed thousands more procedures for decades.

Up until 1945, Freeman had not personally performed the lobotomies, but that was about to change.[70] Looking for a faster and less invasive way to perform the lobotomies, Freeman adopted Amarro Fiamberti's transorbital (entry above the eye) lobotomy and perfected it, using an instrument similar to an ice pick that was hammered into each frontal lobe through the back of each eye socket. Freeman's procedure came to be known as ice pick lobotomy.[71] This grotesque procedure was quick—about ten minutes—and easy for Freeman, or anyone, to perform outside of an operating room without surgical training, essential for Freeman because he was a neurologist, not a surgeon.

In *Forgotten Dead of St. Elizabeth's*, Kelly Patricia O'Meara writes:

> *Freeman's lobotomy procedure included knocking a patient out with electric shocks, lifting the eyelids and inserting an "ice-pick-like" instrument through the tear duct. He [Freeman] pierced the skull bone by tapping on the instrument with a surgical hammer, then shoved the pointed steel about an inch into the frontal lobe of the brain and moved its sharp tip back and forth.*[72]

Freeman singlehandedly popularized the lobotomy as a legitimate form of psychosurgery. He traveled across the country teaching doctors how to perform the procedure, exponentially expanding the use of the lobotomy procedure in state mental hospitals, and in the process, his own notoriety.

Clearly, Dr. Freeman believed that lobotomy would be shown to be successful. But it would be *how* Freeman measured his success that lifted eyebrows and raised many questions about the procedure itself. Edward Shorter, medical historian, says on PBS' *American Experience*:

> *Freeman's definition of success is that the patients were no longer agitated. That doesn't mean they were cured, that means they could be discharged from the asylum, but they were incapable of carrying on normal social life.*[73]

Nolan Lewis, professor of psychiatry at Columbia University

and Director of the New York State Psychiatric Institute in the 1940s, raised his objections to the practice of lobotomy in 1949:

> *Is quieting a patient a cure? Perhaps all it accomplishes is to make things more convenient for those who have to nurse them...the patients become rather childlike...they are as dull as blazes. It disturbs me to see the number of zombies that these operations turn out...I think it should be stopped.*[74]

Evaluating the success of lobotomies (for the ones who survived the operation) was difficult unless you consider babbling speech, vacant empty eyes, and just sitting quietly a measure of success. Many remained in a vegetative state for the rest of their life. They often suffered permanent brain damage and were reduced to a dependent state. But Dr. Freeman ignored the troubling side effects and continued to crusade for the lobotomy. As Jack El-Hai says in *The Lobotomist*:

> *[Freeman] felt certain that lobotomy could return psychologically disabled people, many of whom had no other prospect of effective medical treatment and who lived in oppressive psychiatric wards, to useful lives.*[75]

The young Kennedy girl was just one of many botched lives; there were thousands. Dr. Freeman estimated that lobotomy benefited only 33% of patients that underwent it and 67% were no better off or even worse after the lobotomy. Dr. Freeman knew what was included in that failure rate—people with hemorrhages, seizures, infections and death—but Freeman remained undaunted. Freeman continued to endorse and promote the radical procedure in spite of tragic evidence to the contrary. Apparently 33% was his definition of success. There were doubts it was even that high.[76]

A major study evaluating the results of lobotomy was conducted in the United States and published in 1947, called the Columbia-

Greystone project. The findings: a surprising failure to differentiate between the behavior of the operated and the control patients.[77] In other words, no scientific evidence showing benefits from lobotomy was found.[78]

Even in light of overwhelming proof, like a drunk in an alcohol-induced blackout, Dr. Walter Freeman did not slow the pace of the destructive procedure. He was reported having performed 228 transorbital lobotomies in just a two-week period in 1952 in West Virginia, through a state-sponsored lobotomy project dubbed "Operation Ice Pick" by newspapers.[79]

Dr. Thomas C. Knapp was superintendent at one of the West Virginia hospitals at the time of Freeman's surgical spree. After watching Freeman in action, Knapp's reaction, published in an October 22, 1980 interview in the *Charleston Gazette*, was: "I was never convinced that the operation was helpful and it appeared to me we were dealing with a sadistic bastard." Knapp called it a "grim time for our profession" and said that if long-term follow-up was done, the number who actually improved would be practically zero.[80]

Dr. Walter Freeman performed so many lobotomies that he was nicknamed the "ice pick doctor." A hospital in Santa Monica, California, even has his name on it. Now if becoming financially successful was Freeman's measure of lobotomy success, he made it big time. Freeman performed nearly 3,500 lobotomies himself in 23 states, a staggering number of lives affected, especially considering the only proof of its effectiveness and long-term success came from flawed research.

Most amazing to me is that not one person was able to put a halt to the procedure for over 40 years. Not one of the extremely powerful Kennedys—they were silent. Joe did not want the stigma of mental illness in the Kennedy family to ruin the rest of the family's political aspirations. None of the staff or doctors in the private hospitals or the state hospitals at the time was able to alert the world to the truth.

Freeman's arrogance and blind focus on performing surgeries, no matter how poor the results, how many lives lost or how terrible the side effects, has striking parallels to today's removal of genitals to change genders. Both had scientific studies early on that showed no improvement in the majority of patients' lives. Both had vocal opposition from doctors, which they ignored. Both defined success in their own way and disregarded horrific side effects.

German philosopher Friedrich Hegel said, "The only thing we learn from history is that we learn nothing from history."[81] The frontal lobotomy should have taught us about employing surgical techniques that are irreversible and have the potential to destroy lives, but it has not. Lobotomies changed low functioning people into simple apathetic objects who just stared off into space and needed care for the rest of their lives.

Gender surgery is irreversible and changes people, too. After surgery, they are neither man nor women but plastic surgical configurations of male or female that do not fit into either world. They commit suicide and/or regret the surgery. Some, after many years, want to return to their birth gender even though, sadly, their genitalia no longer match that gender.

Remember the 1979 study at Johns Hopkins that evaluated the results of the first ten or so years of gender surgeries performed under the direction of Dr. John Money? It concluded:

> *To say that this type of surgery cures psychiatric disturbance is incorrect. We now have objective evidence that there is **no real difference** (emphasis added) in the transsexual's adjustment to life in terms of jobs, educational attainment, marital adjustment and social stability.*[82]

Yet, the radical, irreversible, life-changing gender surgery has grown in acceptance and in use as treatment for depression and mental disorders over the ensuing decades. Amazing how its progress mirrors the practice of lobotomy. Even with the prevalence of suicides, alcoholism, drug addiction, regret and disappointment that follows gender change surgery, it continues to be heralded as the treatment of choice. Just like they did with the lobotomy years ago, the very practitioners of the treatment are the ones defining success so that serious side effects aren't considered, and the media cooperates to glamorize the wonder and success of the treatment. Activists and doctors loudly campaign to expand the use of the treatment and discourage any other form of intervention for gender issues.

Some gender change surgeries result in cosmetic masterpieces, with results that many women would envy. Others produce cartoon-like women: clumsy, large and manly-looking. But looks should not be the measure of success. No matter how good the person looks or how well he or she is able to pass as the opposite gender, the surgery does not resolve the underlying psychological disorders.

It seems the providers cannot bring themselves to acknowledge any negative consequences. They carefully define success so that it puts their results in the most positive light. Or, they neglect to track the results of the treatments in any meaningful way over the course of the patients' lives. We never learn how many died, or how many were worse off after such radical surgeries, or how many would have been better off if the doctors did nothing. This is good for the advocates but obviously not helpful for the patients.

Today, the medical treatment of gender issues has been corrupted by a small, but vocal, contingent of political transgender activists. Skeptics keep silent, intimidated by the threat of angry rants if the doubts are made public. The activists have a history of attacking any and all who disagree with them. The first offensive is name-calling. You're a homophobe and a bigot. You are brain-dead, intellectually-challenged, intolerant and insensitive. The gender change activists vocally denounce any treatment but hormones and surgery. They say "no" to medication or long-term psychotherapy. Surgery is the answer, the only answer.

But the truly intolerant are the transgender activist themselves who do not want to acknowledge the truth. To claim gender change success you must exclude suicides, regret, disappointment, medical problems and the ones who abandon their surgical gender and return to living as their birth genders. The activists have infiltrated the scientific community so that research studies aren't framed in a way to acknowledge or study the downsides of gender change treatment.

The patients themselves are intimidated into silence if they ever realize the treatment didn't work for them. "Females" return to their male gender after having gender surgery and receiving female birth records. They stay silent because of their shame and fear of bullying from activists. They are not counted and they do not count. Like the lobotomy patients of the past, it appears that gender change patients are considered throwaway lives by the promoters of the procedure.

The procedure has dubious success rates and suspiciously high suicide rates, yet the pace of activism quickens and gender treatments continue. To continue to perform irreversible surgery over so many decades without adequate study and reporting of the negative side effects is reckless indeed.

Lobotomist Freeman was brilliant in manipulating the media. *The New York Times* ran a story about him proclaiming the advent of a new operation pioneered by a Washington, D.C. scientist that "eased…abnormal worry, apprehension, anxiety, sleeplessness, and nervous tension."[83] Today the media heaps praise on gender change specialists and glamorizes the results.

Over time, Dr. Freeman expanded his criteria for performing lobotomies. He once said, "I won't touch them unless they are faced with disability or suicide." But as time went on, perhaps faced with the reality of the failures, he revised his criteria. He began advocating early intervention, saying, "It is safer to operate than to wait."[84] Sounds familiar, doesn't it? Dr. Spack says the same about gender change for children.

One example of Freeman's relaxed criteria is the 1960 case of a twelve year-old boy, Howard Dully. In his memoir, *My Lobotomy*, Dully, now 56, says, "I remember having big black swollen eyes one day and staying in the hospital for a few days because apparently I had an infection."[85] Freeman did the procedure, not out of medical need, but because Dully's stepmother asked him to perform the surgery. Dully was lobotomized before any other treatment or medication was tried.[86]

Dully has questions for Freeman we should all pay attention to when considering young people for radical procedures: "Why did you go that far when it was plainly evident to the rest of the world that it was not a good thing? Why did you continue?"[87]

Dully also has questions for those in authority who silently observe the nightmare:

> *The sad thing is, the authorities were there. My family had been in contact with any number of doctors. I had been seen by, or Lou [my stepmother] had consulted with, the Santa Clara County Family Services people, the experts in child mental health from Langley Porter, and the state mental health officers at Napa State Hospital. Some of them knew I was going to have a lobotomy. All of them knew Freeman was conducting lobotomies on children. Sometimes they protested after the fact, like they did the day Freeman took me and the other kids to Langley Porter to show us off. But why wasn't anyone taking steps to make sure Freeman wasn't operating on any more children? Why was this allowed to continue?[88]*

In the same way today, we silently stand by while the gender change treatment expands to children. Dr. Spack says the best results are gained by treating patients before they go through puberty. He tells parents to treat children in pre-adolescence with hormone blockers, and in later adolescence with cross-gender hormone therapy and surgery. The parents go along.

Will we see Howard Dully's message to Freeman echoed by today's generation of gender-changed young people, later asking Dr. Spack: "Why the early intervention treatments on 12 year olds? Why did you go that far when the research studies said it was not a good thing to do?" By the time the children reach later adulthood and realize that their lives were taken from them by the procedure, Dr. Spack will be dead and gone and not around to answer the question.

It is difficult to tell the difference between the insanity of the asylum patients from the insanity of the physician who would plunge an ice pick into someone's brain. How about the practice of cutting off a man's genitals or injecting a ten-year-old boy with powerful drugs to stop the natural development of male puberty? Who is sicker, the patient or the doctor?

The drooling of the media over such radical surgeries has showered the surgeons with professional status, prestige, and wealth. Apparently the doctors are like vultures that prey upon the most psychologically distressed.

Freeman benefitted from a media willing to make him look like a brilliant rock star. Today we see Mark who became Dr. Marci Bowers, a transsexual him/herself now performing gender surgery in the San Francisco Bay Area. She is equal to Freeman in her relationship with the media and has that rock star status. We see Dr. Spack at a children's gender clinic in Boston expanding the criteria for gender change and saying "The earlier, the better," helping boys and girls switch genders. Is Dr. Spack the next media star?

The lobotomy procedure only started fading when prescription drug therapies begin to enter the market. Psychiatric doctors could write a prescription to deal with anxiety and depression. The tide was turning and surgical intervention with the lobotomy procedure was on its way out.[89] What will stop the gender changers?

The 40-year history of lobotomy gives us a glimpse into how long it can take to determine the true results when surgery is used as treatment for psychological disorders. Dr. Walter Freeman's frontal lobotomy produced zombie-like people. This was not a novel or a movie; this was the real stuff.

In his time, Freeman was the most recognized and well-respected psychosurgeon in the United States, all without having had surgical training. His practice of plunging an ice pick into an eye socket and randomly digging around in the brain was well known, documented, and freely shared by Freeman himself, yet he was not considered a quack until decades later. Dr. Freeman received front page prominence and acclaim by the print media even though his success was arguably very limited.

Dr. Freeman died in 1972. But the lobotomy procedure continued to be performed through 1986, leaving a tragic trail of over 40,000 people who had undergone the frontal lobotomy.[90]

In *The Lobotomist*, Jack El-Hai describes Freeman this way:

> *Aside from Nazi doctor Josef Mengele, Walter J. Freeman ranks as the most scorned physician of the twentieth century. The operation Freeman refined and promoted, lobotomy, still maintains a uniquely infamous position in the public mind nearly seventy years after its introduction and a quarter-century past its disappearance.*[91]

The New Lobotomy?
Deep Brain Stimulation

Dr. Freeman is gone. Today, psychosurgery has been resurrected with a new brain surgery called Deep Brain Stimulation that is gaining in popularity. Is this the new 21st century lobotomy? And is it really medically necessary?

The stimulation of the brain is achieved by surgically implanting very thin wires in targeted areas deep in the patient's brain, placing a medical device which generates electrical impulses under the skin usually near the collarbone, and connecting them together with a wire under the skin.

Deep Brain Stimulation is in its early stages, medically speaking. It received Food and Drug Administration (FDA) approval as a therapy for movement-related problems associated with essential tremor in 1997 and Parkinson's disease in 2002.

It seemed important to talk to a patient who had undergone the Deep Brain Stimulation surgery. A high school classmate, Gail, underwent the procedure in San Francisco in June 2008. She was willing to do a phone interview for the book.

Gail, a female between the age of 65 and 70, reported that the Deep Brain Stimulation surgical procedure did resolve the tremors from her Parkinson's disease. She feels better because the tremors are not aggravating her any more. She also reported some downsides. She thinks that the procedure accelerated or hastened some normal effects of Parkinson's, like balance and walking ability. Her feet "freeze" and falling has become a problem. Now, she uses a cane for assistance to prevent falling and to keep her balance. A cane was not required prior to the procedure. Gail also reports a noticeable loss of energy. She describes herself as lethargic and says, "I feel the need to push through that." She feels this also came as result of the procedure. It should be noted the conditions she described could be normal progressive changes as a result of Parkinson's. Her speech was noticeably slurred, not quite as crisp or quick as it was in the past.

The Mayo Clinic (mayoclinic.com) is in agreement with Gail's experience: "Side effects are generally mild and reversible. The most common are a temporary tingling in the limbs, slight paralysis, slurred speech and loss of balance."

The success of Deep Brain Stimulation in treating tremors has encouraged medical researchers to examine what other illnesses might be treated. Now the researchers are trying it on patients with mental disorders, such as obsessive-compulsive disorder and treatment-resistant depression. The question is: How reckless is it to start expanding the treatments to other disorders without the completion of long-term studies? After all, it involves placing electrodes into the brain. Any surgical procedure carries risks. But Deep Brain Stimulation involves *brain* surgery, making it especially risky.

But like lobotomy, the proposed extension targets people whose illness isn't helped by conventional treatment. Sarah Richards in her article, "Neurostimulation / Is it a good idea to drill holes in people's heads to treat them for depression?" says,

> *"As invasive and Frankenstein-ish as it may seem, deep brain stimulation…may offer real hope for the 20 percent of depressed Americans whom Prozac can't help."*[92]

Optimistic results early on give new treatments a foothold, but the long-term consequences will not be known until later. Will we see broken and damaged lives because of Deep Brain Stimulation, as happened with Dr. Freeman's lobotomies and Dr. Money's gender surgery, when it is used to treat psychological and mental problems? Just a question.

Summary

The majority of lobotomy patients did not do well—some died, some were paralyzed and many were left childlike and devoid of personality.

"What did success mean in [Freeman's] mind? Mainly it meant getting them out of hospital, these people who returned home from the hospital came home with severe disabilities from their lobotomies," says Jack El-Hai.[93]

Success is measured for transgenders in a similar fashion. The surgical treatment removes them from reality, that is, the real need for psychological or psychiatric help, to a childlike place of fantasy where no reality exists. Transgenders living in their fabricated persona avoid getting the treatment they really need. They escape reality by practicing extreme denial.

The media plays a major role in sensationalizing new surgical procedures as "genius" and "amazing breakthrough" while ignoring or downplaying the stories of patients who are harmed.

It is, no doubt, important for doctors to engage in research to discover and perfect new treatments that improve the quality of life for people who suffer from illness. But we must demand that the horrifying consequences of reckless treatment are reported and that the results are tracked in an objective way over a period of time.

We can learn lessons from studying the example of lobotomy: How do we define success; what role does the media play; who is driving the popularity of the treatment; where are the long-term scientific objective studies and what are the long-term side effects.

We can apply these lessons to evaluate surgeries being promoted as treatment today for psychological problems. And especially for gender disorders, we can begin the process of offering much better results for those who suffer, and keep the body parts where they belong, attached and functional, with few exceptions.

Chapter 4.

Great Balls of Cotton

We've talked about the doctors who are surgically obsessed with genitals and others who loved poking around at brain tissue. Both attempt to treat psychological disorders and become the nation's next media super star. The obsession with psychosurgery and headlines started before Freeman's rise to fame. In the early 1900s the psychosurgery obsession was flourishing at the New Jersey State Hospital at Trenton and the doctor in charge was well on his way to appearing in the headlines of *The New York Times*.

Psychiatrist Dr. Henry Cotton (1876-1933) recklessly experimented on the patients in his care, gained fame and fortune, and ignored the numerous tragic outcomes in the early part of the 20th century. Cotton literally pulled out teeth, often every tooth, in an effort to cure mental illness. When that didn't work, he got even more radical. Sound familiar? Cotton literally slashed his way into medical infamy by removing teeth and cutting away at other organs inside the body cavity.[94]

Dr. Cotton's chief mentor and good friend was none other than Dr. Adolf Meyer, the head of the Johns Hopkins University psychiatry department. As we have already seen, the prominent Dr.

Meyer would come to the aid of Dr. Freeman at a crucial moment in 1936, thereby launching the age of lobotomy. Dr. Meyer believed the solutions for mental health problems were to be found in surgery. He strongly influenced the practice of psychiatry for decades, pushing the field away from psychoanalysis talk therapy toward surgery.

When the New Jersey State Hospital at Trenton (now known as the Trenton Psychiatric Hospital) was casting about for a new medical director, Dr. Meyer strongly recommended his former student, 30 year old Dr. Cotton for this plum assignment. Later on, Dr. Meyer would personally cover up Cotton's failures and allow his wildly destructive surgical treatment to continue.

Whatever possessed Dr. Cotton to consider teeth as the cause of mental illness? In Cotton's day, the sexually transmitted disease syphilis was virtually untreatable, and it was thought to cause a most deadly mental disorder, General Paralysis of the Insane. In 1913, a major breakthrough occurred—the discovery of the bacterium that causes syphilis. Dr. Cotton got caught up in all the excitement in the medical and scientific communities over the science of bacteria and infection.

Cotton quickly concluded that *all* mental illnesses were caused by infections, based on his observations that patients with high fever became delusional or hallucinated. Looking at this through the lens of our time, this may seem absurd. But at the time, the study of bacteria and infection was new and promising and everyone was jumping on the bandwagon. Dr. Cotton simply made the leap from *one* disorder being caused by infection to *all* mental illnesses being caused by infection.

Cotton thought if he could rid the patients of the infections, then he could cure them of their mental illness. Dr. Cotton became convinced his theory was right. And as time went on, not even overwhelming evidence of his failures would shake his conviction. He was on a mission.

Today, gender surgeons and the approving therapists make a

similar leap. They say that surgery is the answer to *every* gender issue. Just like in Cotton's case, the treatment is unproven yet promoted as true, before adequate medical review is done.

Cotton's first target was teeth, initially only those showing signs of infection. His weakness, though, like that of many enthusiasts, was that he did not know when to stop. If teeth were not already infected, they might be later, so it was safer to remove them all. Bad teeth would obviously infect saliva, which he believed would carry toxins into the digestive tract.[95]

Stomachs, colons, even reproductive organs and testicles weren't exempt from removal. Some patients were maimed beyond recognition and barely alive at all. Many patients survived the surgery only to die soon after from infections caused by the surgery.[96]

Dr. Cotton used his position of authority as director of the mental hospital to force patients to undergo the theoretical procedures. He convinced their families of the value of the procedure and with family (not patient) consent, he proceeded with surgery. Some patients were literally dragged, kicking and screaming, into the operating room so that the "treatment" could begin.[97]

The medical community's historic duty is "Do no harm." Clearly, Cotton was practicing a different creed: better to do *something* than nothing, even if it kills the patient. Cotton did not think he was reckless. He was convinced that his approach would not only cure people who were psychologically distressed, but would also prevent afflictions from developing. Fact is, doing something rather than nothing is often bad medicine.

Cotton put his theory of infection as the cause of insanity into practice on a wide variety of mental health issues. The problem was that no one, including Dr. Cotton or Professor Meyer knew how to prevent mental illness or what caused it (medicine today doesn't know either). Cotton and Meyer were both wrong; in some cases, dead wrong.

Dr. Cotton publicly claimed a cure rate in excess of 80% for his treatment procedures.[98] He later admitted that he included in the success rate *the ones who died* from the treatment, saying they were no longer suffering from the illness. Unfortunately, when the surgeons themselves set the standards for success, they often succumb to the temptation to tip the scales in their favor.

Tireless in his zeal, Cotton promoted his treatment in every way. He wrote medical journal articles and made formal presentations at professional meetings. He cultivated relationships with prestigious members of the medical and university communities and traveled to other mental institutions to proclaim the cure. Cotton invited the president of the American Medical Association to tour Trenton Hospital and see his treatment program. After visiting, the president endorsed Cotton's approach.[99]

Thanks to sponsorship by two influential Princeton faculty members, Cotton was invited to give a series of lectures at Princeton. Taking full advantage of this extremely prestigious platform, he presented the case for his theories and included 25 case histories that demonstrated dramatic recovery. When the lectures were published in book form, his mentor Adolf Meyer wrote a glowing forward.[100]

The New York Times elevated Dr. Cotton to high esteem in the review of the book, calling his leadership brilliant:

> *At the State Hospital at Trenton, N.J., under the brilliant leadership of the medical director, Dr. Henry A. Cotton, there is on foot the most searching, aggressive, and profound scientific investigation that has yet been made of the whole field of mental and nervous disorders...there is hope, high hope...for the future.*[101]

Cotton's treatments were in high demand. In the book the *Tale of Two Villages*, Michael Nevins tells us that after the newspaper publicity made Cotton a star, the wealthy wanted Dr. Cotton's "cure" and flocked to make appointments for the treatment. The hospital in Trenton was soon filled with rich private patients.[102]

Dr. Cotton saw dollar signs and opened his own private hospital to treat wealthy clients. Cotton filled his bank account with large sums of money earned by removing teeth and organs. People are no smarter today than they were in the 1920s, willing to risk their own life or their kids' lives on unproven experimental medical procedures, trusting glowing headlines and passionate doctors in a medical version of Russian roulette.

Unfortunately, we only learned of the death, carnage and recklessness in hindsight. Between 1918 and 1925, 2,186 major operations were performed at the Trenton hospital. It was not limited to patients suffering from psychosis; they were done on children to correct "sexual abnormalities" such as masturbation, in order to prevent insanity.[103] Dr. Cotton was experimenting on people without knowing or considering the long-term consequences, and he did it over a long period of time. Only now, we know he destroyed many lives practicing his theories in his attempt to cure psychological distress.

Some in the medical community challenged Dr. Cotton's treatments and eventually called for an independent investigation. Dr. Cotton agreed to the investigation but somehow he finagled to have the "unbiased" investigation overseen by his former professor and friend, Dr. Adolph Meyer.

The report of Cotton's success rate was completed in 1925 and the news was devastating. The true recovery rate was no more than 32%, or in other words, a 68% failure rate. Among the many ill effects of Cotton's drastic treatment was an eye-popping post-operative mortality rate for those who had their colons cut: 45% died from complications of the surgery.[104]

The devastating results were never published. Very simply, Dr. Adolf Meyer withheld the findings, and made no attempt to restrain his friend Cotton from performing the radical surgeries. Meyer knew without a doubt the death rate from Cotton's radical treatments was unacceptably high, yet he hushed up the report which would have discredited the practice. Dr. Adolph Meyer is the same man who later would come to Freeman's rescue at the medical conference in 1936 that launched 40 years of the lobotomy procedure.

It is understandable why Meyer would protect Dr. Cotton and not be willing to disclose the distressing findings. He was Cotton's mentor, friend and supporter, and as the medical community knew, Meyer was the source of the original infection theory. If any failures with Cotton's treatment became widely known, Meyer's own esteem and prestige would potentially have suffered along with Dr. Henry Cotton's.

Even in the face of overwhelming evidence, Cotton did not change his conviction that his procedures worked in the treatment of mental illness. He even went so far as to remove his own teeth when he felt his illness merited it.[105] But he stopped there. He did not remove his colon or his testicles. Today gender change surgeon Mark/Marci Bowers not only had his own testicles removed, but has gone on to make a living removing the testicles of other men, claiming to have changed them from male to female. How many will be happy in 20 years is unknown.

While Dr. Cotton was removing the testicles of his patients, he symbolically did the same with his medical colleagues and the patients' families, even *The New York Times*. Even after Cotton's untimely death in 1933, his recommended treatment protocol of pulling teeth and removing body parts continued at the hands of those he had trained.[106] No one was able to stop the procedures until the State of New Jersey stepped in.

Summary

Like Dr. Freeman, Dr. Money and Dr. Biber, Dr. Cotton ignored the failures of his treatment. He knew the surgical procedures had poor success rates, yet continued to perform the surgeries anyway.

What is so instructive about Dr. Cotton is he kept on cutting away.

We see that medical prestige and glowing news reports often hide the horror of broken lives, failures and suicides. We learn that doctors will hide or suppress negative outcomes like Dr. Adolph Meyer did for Cotton. We see that researchers will report failures as success, like Cotton did with patients' deaths and Freeman did with lobotomies.

Gender surgeons today testify that gender change has a very high rate of success by failing to include the suicides, regret, medical problems and those who return to their birth gender. Researchers and doctors will hide facts, twist the results and hide failures from their peers and the public in order to protect their practice and prestige.

Meanwhile, the lives of patients are irreparably damaged.

Chapter 5.

No Medical Necessity

Anyone has the right to undergo elective or cosmetic surgery on his or her own body. But we as taxpayers should object when we are expected to pay for it in some way, such as through taxes or insurance premiums.

Is the gender surgery medically necessary? The definition of medically necessary is treatment that is absolutely necessary to protect the health of the patient and if withheld could adversely affect the patient's condition.[107]

The activists say sex change surgery is as much a medical necessity as treatment for diabetes or high blood pressure.[108] Really, high blood pressure and diabetes equal to gender surgery? Let's be real—the gender surgery is only cosmetic. It hardly rises to the level of medically necessary.

One way to arrive at an answer is to look at court rulings. I would assume that if the medical necessity of the surgery had been proven, the courts would order that it be given to prisoners, for example. If a prisoner were denied surgery to remove a ruptured appendix, they would die. Not so easy to see in the case of gender disorders.

The State of Massachusetts Correctional Department claimed

the gender surgery was not medically necessary in the 2006 trial concerning Michelle, formerly Robert, Kosilek, age 57. Kosilek is serving life in prison for murdering his wife.

Corrections officials say their decision to deny the surgery has nothing to do with costs or the politics of crime. They cite the testimony of their experts and Kosilek said that the feelings of depression have diminished since taking hormones.[109]

Gay, lesbian, bisexual and transgender (GLBT) advocates have taken up Kosilek's cause, and are on a mission to help all cross gender prisoners benefit from state-paid gender operations. The Lambda Legal Group, a gay- and transgender-rights group, pleaded the case on behalf of Kosilek. They say that the proof of medical necessity is that Kosilek had attempted suicide twice.

Both sides brought in medical experts. As you would expect, doctors arguing for Kosilek said they believe the surgery is medically necessary for Kosilek, while the experts for the Correction Department concluded Kosilek does not need gender surgery.[110]

Although testimony in this case ended over three years ago, the judge has given no indication when he will rule. Other transgender inmates across the country have sued prison officials wanting surgery, but none as of this date has persuaded a judge to order a state-financed sex change operation. Apparently, no compelling medical evidence has shown that the surgery fulfills the definition of medically necessary.

Cases like Kosilek's cast great doubt about the urgency and the necessity for gender surgery. If the prisoner had a real medical necessity for surgery, he wouldn't need a gay activist group to argue his case in court. The long delay to rule in itself demonstrates that the Department of Corrections proved it was not a medical necessity.

Is this like AIDS, where people are dying and research is lagging? Yes. People are dying, but not for lack of surgery. Transgenders are dying from lack of research to discover the true treatment for their ailment. With AIDS, the activists put their efforts toward exposing the lack of quality research and treatment. But for gender disorders, the activists are not advocating for more research that could lead to an effective treatment, they only push for surgery and they loudly scorn any medical findings to the contrary.

Why would an advocate group use their efforts to push for the government to pay for cosmetic surgery for inmates rather than lobbying the medical community to find the cause of the illness? Their focus is on changing laws to promote and protect certain types of sexual activity and on growing their political base by any means necessary. The logical conclusion is that ensuring effective medical and psychological treatments for transgenders doesn't matter as much as having more people go through the unnecessary, irreversible surgery. They gain more power by growing their membership.

We saw in the Kosilek case that the Department of Corrections was providing the prisoner with female hormone therapy (known to reduce anxiety in men) but drew the line at gender surgery, and the court has not overturned that decision. In the next case, we see a federal judge striking down part of a 2005 Wisconsin law, the Inmate Sex Change Prevention Act, which prohibits prison inmates from getting hormone therapy or surgery to treat gender identity disorder.

Three transgender prisoners sued because inmates with other ailments were allowed to have hormone therapy based on the recommendation of their doctors, but they were not. In March, 2010, the U.S. District judge found that the law unconstitutional on its face and also in violation of the inmates' rights to equal protection.[111]

"We're very excited about it," said Laurence Dupuis, legal director of the ACLU of Wisconsin Foundation, which with Lambda Legal (a gay advocacy group) represented the three named plaintiffs in the case. Though the judge's ruling doesn't address surgery, only hormone therapy, Dupuis said he thinks the ruling supports the principle that any medical care in prisons must be based on medical judgment, which means the surgery would at least be theoretically possible.[112] The point here is the activists will not stop at hormone therapy and will continue pushing for correctional institutions to pay for medically unnecessary genital reconstruction unless someone stops them with laws specifically preventing it.

Some understand that using taxpayer dollars for sex reassignment surgery for prisoners is foolishness, as we see in this Canadian example. In 2010, Canadian Public Safety Minister Vic Toews instructed the Correctional Service of Canada (CSC) to stop performing sex reassignment surgery for transgender federal inmates. Toews said, "The courts have ruled that CSC must provide essential medical services to inmates. However, we do not believe that sex change surgery is an essential medical service or that Canadian taxpayers should pay for sex change surgery for criminals."[113]

In the United States, as far back as 1967, the American Civil Liberties Union (ACLU) has been bringing discrimination lawsuits on behalf of transgender people. They pledge on their website to advocate for gender identity inclusion in state, federal, and local anti-discrimination policies.[114] If they fail to force taxpayers to pay for gender surgery with the argument of "medically necessary," just wait and see, the ACLU will try other arguments to achieve it, such as anti-discrimination policy.

We can see elements of their political agenda in an excerpt of a speech at the TRANScending Gender Symposium held in Boulder, Colorado, on November 7, 2008. The theme of the symposium was "The Future of Transgender Activism." Keynote speaker, trans-woman Barbara Jordan, said, "This is an interesting time to have a conference. We are now roughly 72 hours past a historic election in which an African-American will be occupying the Oval Office on January 20…the best part is that Barack Hussein Obama will be picking the Supreme Court justices when the next openings on the court happen." That is their political agenda—the passage of new laws protecting a wide range of sexual activity. The symposiums are frequently held to promote ways to expand sexual rights and develop protection from prosecution for having sex with young people.[115]

Interviews by the Author

I shared with you in the early part of the book that I had spoken to some of the key leaders in the gender surgery movement, well-respected medical professionals who know the effectiveness and impact of gender change. I spoke with them at different times over the years and in a nutshell, their surprising answers are as follows. Each makes his own case and all are different.

Dr. John Money in the late 1980s

Dr. John Money was instrumental in opening the Johns Hopkins Gender Clinic in 1966. I spoke with him in the late 1980s. Money said to me, "The continuation of hormone therapy is above all the greatest factor in determining and maintaining the gender change. While the surgery is important, you can identify and live female without the surgical procedure. If you are a male having genital surgery and stop taking the female hormones, you are no longer a female. Taking hormones is the key after the surgery to maintaining the transition from male to female."

Dr. Stanley Biber in 1981 and 1983

Dr. Biber had pioneered and performed nearly 3,000 surgeries by the time of my first interview with him in 1981. Biber was not very engaging during my interview at the bank building in Trinidad, Colorado. When I asked about failures Biber was quick to distance himself from any responsibility and said, "I let the psychologists determine someone's fitness for the gender surgery. This is why I require a letter form a psychologist approving the surgery prior to my hospital surgical procedure." One thing that struck me was my first look at his office. Frankly, it looked to me like a set from the movie *One Flew over the Cuckoo's Nest*, old and dingy like a mental hospital—what a good clue.

I spoke to Dr. Biber again in 1983. He shared with me that he was confident that he was performing a great service to the transgender community by providing surgery. Biber felt the surgical genital procedure was the key to living as a female. He said, "The hormones are important but you cannot perform as a female without the surgical changes." Sexual performance, that is, having the equipment to act as a female in a sexual way, was most important in Dr. Biber's mind.

Dr. Paul Walker in the 1980s

I interviewed Dr. Paul Walker in his Union Street office three times during the 1980s. Over a period of about six years we exchanged letters and notes with our thoughts and views regarding failures and the approval process.

Dr. Walker was a homosexual psychologist, and a strong advocate for gender surgery. He admitted to me that he regretted approving at least one or more surgeries when he was under the influence of prescription medication and alcohol. He told me that his addiction came as a result of a spiral leg break. He claimed he was being open and transparent with me as part of his recovery, that admitting when he was wrong was a way toward healing.

Walker came with a different perspective on gender change than either Money or Biber. Walker thought the key to success in changing genders was not hormones or surgery but the adaptability to living in a new gender role without collapsing under all the stress and difficulty that had proven to be too much for many who changed genders. This perspective would be expected from a psychologist, a complete psychological viewpoint.

Dr. Walker was a kind person. I could see he had some regrets from his own past; his recovery and illness made him reflective.

AIDS was taking life from him, one day at a time. Truly in the end, Dr. Paul Walker wanted to make things right and he admitted he had made mistakes in approving some for surgery.

Dr. Paul McHugh in 2009 and 2010

My two telephone interviews with Dr. Paul McHugh occurred in 2009 and 2010. Other contacts were made via email to him at his office at Johns Hopkins.

From 1975 until 2001, McHugh was the Henry Phipps Professor of Psychiatry and the director of the Department of Psychiatry and Behavioral Science at Johns Hopkins University. At one time, he was psychiatrist-in-chief at Johns Hopkins Hospital. He is currently University Distinguished Service Professor of Psychiatry at Johns Hopkins University School of Medicine.

The first time I talked to him, my purpose was to see if anything at all had come along in the thirty plus years since the 1978 report from the Johns Hopkins Gender Clinic to change his mind regarding the ineffectiveness of gender change surgery to treat gender disorder. His response was: "Mr. Heyer, sex change surgery is a disaster. I wish I knew how to fight this craze. I've done my best from a fairly strong position but I've had no success. Only some disaster or some massive court decision can bring it to an end I fear."

McHugh is not liked by the homosexual or transgender advocates because he shut down the surgery program at Johns Hopkins after the study of results showed no difference in the patients' mental health after surgery. Most of the university-affiliated gender clinics in the U.S. followed suit.

Four very key players in the field of gender changing, with a combined one hundred plus years of experience, each espousing a different view of the key factor, and not one making the claim the surgery is medically necessary, not one.

Not one of these medical professionals who were active in the early days of treating transsexuals in the U.S. said surgery was a medically necessity. Only the surgeon Dr. Biber said surgery was even important, and that was only for sexual performance. Perhaps that is telling enough about the medical reality.

Remember, within this group we have arguably the most experienced professionals when it came to surgery for changing genders. Not one of them made the case that gender changing surgery was a medical necessity. Even so, most likely under ObamaCare, taxpayers will be footing the bill for a surgical procedure whose only purpose is to alter genitalia so men can identify as women and do sex differently, and vice versa for the women.

It is crazy when you consider the investment banking giant Goldman Sachs added sex reassignment surgery to their health-insurance coverage as part of an all-out push to attract top talent and recruit and retain a more diverse workforce.[116] Our tax money bailed them out with TARP funds in 2009. Diversity is a key activist word used in conjunction with tolerance.

More focus needs to be placed on patient psychological evaluations. The claim that transgenders are born that way implies that psychological evaluations will not yield results. So, from the activist perspective there is no need to seriously look at possible childhood trauma, abuse or comorbidity; just get them hormones and get them under the knife and they're good to go.

Real Life Stories

The following real life stories are further proof the surgery has no medical necessity. What we see is that gender changing brings with it great regret. Every age is represented by real people whose heart-breaking reactions to surgery are rarely represented in media portrayals.

June 25, 2010

Thank you, Walt,

The work you are doing is very important. It is a shame there is not more data on Female to Male.

I know a very troubled young girl, who, at about age 13, saw a web site on F to M sex change and suddenly decided she had been born the wrong sex. THAT was the cause of all her problems--her social isolation, her obsessions and her continual conflict with her controlling mother. Her mother took her to a prominent sex change therapist in Boston who prescribed testosterone.

She has just turned 18, was just hospitalized for anorexia, and is below the tenth percentile for females in height and weight. She wears a fedora and tie and has this peculiar beard on her tiny frame.

Those few who can pull off the sex change masquerade may fair well enough in their new roles but this poor girl is a grotesque caricature of a man. It is so sad. None of her problems have been solved. They have only gotten worse.

The next email comes from one who regrets the surgical procedure, but is happy with hormone therapy.

October 26, 2010

Walt,

First of all, have you met anyone like me? Regrets the surgery but not the hormones or social transition? Second - what about trying to get some doctors who want to actually put things right with us? Whether it's just getting a penis back or helping to make someone who transitioned from male to female back to male?

I emailed you once before. It was my fault. Not my therapist's. Not the surgeon's.

That said, I still feel bad and I feel like there is nowhere to turn. The entire trans "community" from the doctors to the therapists to the other trans people I felt have turned their backs on me. They don't want to help. They just want me to go away.

This is a real issue with the activist homosexual, lesbian and transgender community turning their back on regretters, unless you walk in lock step with their views, they will even bully you f....off and scorn and ridicule you and they say they get bullied, yea.

I, too, have found the activists to be the biggest bullies of all toward anyone who opposes the surgery, launching the F-bomb—a nice way to show gay pride.

The following person encourages me to keep up the good work, so I will.

June 13, 2010

Hi Walt,

Thanks for your site. You are very brave. A fresh breeze of common sense, you present a welcome caution and note of reality to the sea of gender dysphoria out there. I always find it interesting on the TV when men decide to come out as a 'woman' but look confused and hurt. But as you testify we are men and that is what we are, and we cannot change it, so why bother entering into the world of woman-ness at all? I think a lot of guys, if they heard you, would shake off the daydream, and stop going down that road, knowing that they can never be a woman, so let's get on with the business of being what we are- simply male!

Sincerely, (name withheld)

Another email from someone who understands I want to provide help for the regretters.

May 19, 2010

Walt;

Thank you. As a writer, I try to write my books/ stories with the intent of bringing some attention to many silenced groups, and in this case, it is transsexuals who take on gender surgery who experience regret. Most of the sites and sources I have looked at on this subject insist that the people who have regret about this were simply not 'true transsexuals'.

I am glad I found your site, because it gives factual, non biased information, without trying to shove a crusade for gender surgery down my throat. It also does not belittle the people who feel regret, as many other sites do.

Thank you again for the help-

The next email talks about separation anxiety disorder and how it can mimic gender identity disorder where the patient takes on the persona of the person he fears he has lost. We see the person's undiagnosed separation anxiety disorder remains untreated.

October 6, 2010
Walt,

I have borderline personality. I've been around the cross-dressing /ts / gay world for years and have, within the past couple of years, done a good amount of reading. Because the illness is so deeply ingrained however I find that I need to make several, no many, passes over the material to make it seem real. There's been a lot of pain.

I think you're at a place where you must have had exposure to what I'm going thru. I didn't/don't suspect that this has been your personal challenge. My partner, a self-proclaimed ts/tg is attached and has, what I see, as separation anxiety disorder.

This is all a lot, maybe, for you to take in. What do you know, relatively briefly about all this? Thanks.

This one from a distressed wife with a transgender husband—

June 18, 2010

Hello Walt

It's me again; we spoke on the phone a couple of times last year. My husband is being treated for GID. He has legally changed his name to a female name and is taking hormones. By mid-December he will have been on hormones for at least a year.

At the time when we talked first, I was asking you questions about how to protect my girls from him. We are still in a slow divorce process, and I am trying to fight for full custody of my girls.

Walt, please call me if you would be so kind. I really need to pick your brain on some matters that might be able to help my case. Would you please reach out once again, and try to help me.
Signed, Distressed and no place to turn

This brings up an important point. Rarely do we consider the psychological impact on the children or wife when the husband turns to surgery. All too often the family is not prepared for this life-changing event.

Some transgenders think if they just look wonderful all their troubles will be over. Wrong. I have discovered even when the male turned female looks beautiful on the outside, the unseen internal psyche remains confused and troubled.

Most gender failures are not reported but Australian Allen Finch was an exception. His story was featured in a documentary called *Boy Interrupted*, seen on *Australian Story* on September 1, 2003.[117] Alan Finch's decision at 19 to become a woman was supported by health-care professionals as well as his mother. It took him on a journey from which he has painfully discovered there is no sure way back. His original diagnosis of gender identity disorder had been wrong. Alan now understands that what he needed was simple psychotherapy, not sex change surgery. At the age of 30, Alan returned to living as his birth gender, with a mutilated body.

Allen Finch and his psychiatrist say he started down this path in childhood with a lack of a positive father figure. His psychiatrist says, "[Alan] never had any positive role modeling. The whole reason that he attempted to take refuge in womanhood was that he simply couldn't learn from his father how to be anything that he wanted to be." Alan is real-life evidence of how the family environment will affect the hard wiring of the brain.

Alan thought he might have been gay. Then he thought, maybe not. Maybe he was trapped in the wrong body. That is how it starts—internal questioning thoughts that get reinforced by others along the way. In Alan's case, his mother, his girlfriend at the time, and health-care professionals all supported a false idea.

When Alan migrated to Australia with his mother and sister at age nineteen, he saw gender change as an opportunity to truly have a new life. He says of this time, "My focus was to be the best-looking woman I could be. I got a job; I was getting attention from men. I felt powerful." According to Alan, when he didn't pass the pre-surgery psychiatric test the first time, he skewed his answers the next time so that he would qualify for the surgery.

After nine years of living as a woman, during which time he even married a man, Alan started a relationship with a woman and it was there that he came to a positive conclusion to return to his male gender. He says, "I knew with my whole being that was what I wanted to do." He began taking male hormones, something he says now was "a roller-coaster ride emotionally."

Alan was angry at himself for having been so gullible to think that becoming a woman would solve his identity crisis. This is a typical response from regretters—they feel lied to, and they were. As Alan says, "Everything was fake about it, from top to toe."

Allen's views are shared by the growing number of regretters who physically have no way back, their bodies serving as constant reminders of surgery that was never needed. It doesn't take a rocket scientist to figure out why the researchers can't find up to 90% of the transgenders years after surgery. Many revert back to the birth gender (and birth name) and others just opt out of life via suicide.

Many transsexuals are psychologically in need. They push their way into getting approved for surgery, buying into the lie that life will be sunny on the other side. They do not have a clue about the rightness or the wrongness of surgery and do not understand the depth of their psychological disorders.

The activists say that anyone can select a gender. The psychologists could at least caution patients that gender changing is not always the right answer and that surgery can lead to suicide, dissatisfaction, regret, medical problems and a desire to return to one's birth gender. But the activists go ballistic when psychologists tell transgenders the truth. And of course then they do what activists do—they lobby for laws to prohibit psychologists from telling the truth.

Some psychologists hand the diagnostic process over to the clients saying, "I don't know. Only you can know if surgery is right for you." This is wrong on so many levels. It is irresponsible to say "I don't know" and then give the okay for surgery. Shouldn't approval for an irreversible surgery warrant a better diagnosis than this? The lack of proper evaluation and psychoanalysis continues to foster sex change regret.

One Last Example

This last example has all the elements: misdiagnosis, suicide attempts and early childhood experiences that twisted this poor boy's perception of his gender identity into a knot.

The young boy was normal from all accounts until some events begin to alter and reshape his view of who he was. Sometimes when Grandma babysat him alone, she would dress him in female clothing that she made especially for him. His uncle, a troubled teenager, had a favorite sport: making fun of the little boy and yanking down his pants. The uncle turned more aggressive and fondled the boy far too many times over several years, especially while intoxicated.

The young boy started to fantasize about becoming a girl. After years of obsessing, along came Christine Jorgensen in 1955 and the first media reports of a gender change. Then the young boy started to think it was true and he, too, could change genders. The boy in his silence adopted a female name, Cristal West, but only he would know this name and the battleground that was inside him; this silent struggle lasted for years.

Trying to battle against the female trapped inside his body, the boy excelled at all that was male: football, track, cars and yes, girls. All looked normal from the outside, but inside there was pain and confusion about his gender.

As a young teen, the boy attended Eagle Rock Episcopal Church on Chickasaw Avenue. In his teens, the boy sought guidance for his struggle with the internal female from the pastor, Father Carol Barber. At their second meeting, to his shock, Father Barber moved out from behind his desk, unzipped his long black robe to reveal his naked body, and tempted the boy to have homosexual sex. The boy, appalled by the overture, quickly departed and never met with Father Barber again.

In his early twenties, the young man got married, had children and developed skills for high achievement in the business world, first as an aerospace associate design engineer, then by his forties, achieving a national operations position for a major corporation. But his internal struggle with his gender identity never went away and he used alcohol to numb the pain. Alcohol became the pathway to drugs which would bring his impressive career to an abrupt and tragic end.

In his forties, his marriage failed. His two teenage children suffered a great betrayal when their father turned to hormone therapy in San Francisco. A skinny old doctor named Garfield who asked no questions and took no names provided the hormone injections. Over the course of time, Dr. Paul Walker approved him for surgery and Dr. Biber performed the surgical gender change.

In 1983, the man became Laura with a new birth record that specified gender as female. She had success after a few years —good looks and good jobs, recovery from drugs and alcohol—but living as a female just did not resolve the internal struggles. It was during the time Laura was studying to be a counselor at U.C. Santa Cruz in the late 1980s that she came to understand that as a transgender, she was living a self-imposed exile from her true identity.

As Laura's intellect and thought processing ability reemerged from the alcohol- and drug-induced fog, a sober Laura could see that being a transgender was not real, but a fantasy forged out of very powerful obsessive thoughts and feelings that took over her life. As a young boy, the expression he had used to express his feelings of hurt and pain was "girl trapped in a male body." Hiding in a transgender persona was her elaborate way to escape the deep hurt. Acting out was very important to Laura in expressing how she felt, but letting feelings define identity is never a good idea. She later commented that transgender life was like living in a temporary zip code not located near reality. She learned that the transgender feelings would be overwhelming at times, but no matter how strong the feelings are, they can never define her real identity.

Laura was determined to recover on every level, including her male birth gender. She learned in her counseling studies that recovery requires an unwavering persistence with good people supporting her. Recovery was a bit rocky and the path twisted and difficult, but now with 25 years in the rear view mirror, he is restored and has been married to a wonderful lady for 14 years. He made it back.

I know this story all too well, because that was me, the little kid from Glendale. Most of my life I thought I had been born in the wrong body but my traumatic experiences occurred after birth, not in the womb. Regrettably, I learned to dislike the boy who was fondled by an uncle, cross-dressed by a grandmother and propositioned by a homosexual clergyman. I was never a homosexual or felt the desire for men. My rejection of my birth gender was the result of abuse I suffered from several adults.

I learned after surgery that my primary issue was called dissociative identity disorder, which in turn either caused the gender disorder or displayed symptoms that looked like it. The treatment was strenuous psychotherapy to address the primary disorder, not undergoing irreversible surgery to treat a symptom. Comorbidity, the presence of more than one disorder in an individual, is common in transgenders.[118]

So, what made me so different from other transgenders? That is simple—I wanted to recover. Like any recovery, it started with the desire to recover. Without desire, no change is even possible. I did not want to live my life in a masquerade, but in truth. I discovered there was no real medical necessity for the surgery. It was a lie.

Even the doctors who were advocating for me to change genders did not have a clue what it was all about. Psychologist Paul Walker said adaptability is the key to success in changing genders. Surgeon Stanley Biber said success is defined by the ability to physically engage in sex. Psychologist John Money at Johns Hopkins said hormones make the new gender work. Not one, however, said surgery was medical necessary, so it must not be. Dr. Paul McHugh reflects views that more closely align with my personal experience when he said, "It's a disaster." Sadly, a gender wreck is not one you bounce back from easily.

In my view the history of psychosurgery demonstrates a lack of accountability and oversight in the medical community that continues today. Activist lawyers and doctors join together to lobby for, and effectively get, more and more laws passed that provide even more protection for reckless, medically unnecessary surgeries. The evidence suggests a need exists for a broader base of non-surgical therapies, such as psychological interventions, in an effort to improve care.

Now the children have caught the eye of the activist surgeons. Soon young kids will go under the knife and we'll see television shows like "Twelve Year Old Transgenders in Tiaras." Who should hold accountable the doctors who are playing with children's hormones? A 2007 Dutch study says, "Fifty-two percent of the children diagnosed with GID [gender identity disorder] had one or more diagnoses other than GID…Clinicians working with children with GID should be aware of the risk for co-occurring psychiatric problems."[119] Treating GID with irreversible surgery, while ignoring co-existing conditions, is a recipe for patient regret and suicide.

Transgenders want more freedom when perhaps they actually need more boundaries. The real life-threatening harm to transgenders is not a consequence of bullying; it results from the transgenders' own high-risk sexual behaviors,[120] illicit drug use, and alcohol abuse.[121] Transgenders have been shown to be prone to harming themselves. Unfortunately, the activist agenda is directed toward more laws to protect transgenders instead of finding better treatments to reduce the number of suicides and regretters.

The evidence is clear—the surgery is not medically necessary and many problems occur as a result of changing genders. The personal testimonies are further confirmation that changing genders can result in very painful regret. In the next chapter we conclude with an explanation of how effective treatment got derailed by the activists and we explore some possible solutions for reducing the number of transgender regretters and deaths by suicide.

Chapter 6.

Removing the Mask

"In a time of universal deceit telling the truth is a revolutionary act." George Orwell

In writing this book, I was not sure what I would discover. Most of all, I wanted to let the actual objective research studies tell the story. I wanted to learn if the regret I experienced during the first 55 years of my life was an isolated case or the norm. What I found was even more shocking than I had ever thought: the percentages of regret and suicide are quite high even though the advocates make it sound like these rarely happen.

I want to make it clear. I do not want to stop gender surgery. I *do* want to improve how people get approved for surgery in an effort to stop surgeries which are not necessary because those are the ones that result in tragedy.

We started our journey by talking about the radical social changes that evolved as a result of one man, Kinsey who from a young age, in the words of researcher Judith Reisman, was a "violently masochistic masturbation addict" and a sexual predator.[122]

We illustrated some of the colossal failures in psychosurgery over the last 100 years that not only fell woefully short of treating the psychological disorders; they caused great harm and even death. When we examine the origins of treating transsexuals in the U.S., we see transgender doctors Harry Benjamin, John Money and now Norman Spack of Boston Children's Hospital, aligned with Kinsey's homosexual pedophile views. Kinsey's results, based on erroneous research, continue to influence scientific study, public policies, and legislation today in ways which erode the foundations of marriage and family in America.

It is unfortunate—if someone in the medical field scientifically tries to explore the idea that some psychological disorders may exist in transgenders, the GLBT activists become almost militant and view it as an attack on their sexual orientation or on their right to switch genders. Scientific research is, in effect, influenced and even censored by a political faction. As a result, this patient group is not getting the same level of care as the general population.

Denial is the order of the day. The transgenders themselves are encouraged to deny even the possibility that any secondary psychological disorders could co-exist with gender issues. But changing genders can be a symptom of some form of depression. Untreated, depression often results in alcoholism, drug addiction, anger and yes, even suicide.

We saw a prime example of having secondary issues in the last chapter with the prisoner, Michelle, formerly Robert Kosilek, who is suing the Department of Corrections to provide gender surgery. It should not be a big leap to consider a murderer has deep unresolved psychological problems in conjunction with his gender issues.

The objective research suggests that: 1) transgenders are not born that way, 2) secondary issues do exist, and 3) the transgender population is at risk for regret and suicide.

But political activism trumps objective research. Political activism may actually shut down objective research that dares to explore any of these soon-to-become politically-incorrect areas of study.

In the name of political correctness, differing views are silenced, even views based on objective evidence. By insisting on political correctness, activists enjoy unchecked freedom to promote any myth they want.

Homosexuality is one example of where facts are secondary to political correctness and the activist agenda. Think of how often this myth has been repeated: "homosexuals make up 10% of the population." Bruce Voeller of the National Gay Task Force takes credit for the origination of the 10% myth, which he based loosely on Kinsey's data. Voeller says his efforts to promote the number were deliberate. His goal was to expand gay political power by convincing politicians and the public that homosexuals are "everywhere."[123]

The true percentage of homosexuals in the population, based on three objective reports, is less than two people out of a hundred, a fraction of the mythical 10%. The National Health and Social Life Survey (NHSLS) conducts highly-regarded studies on sexual practices in the U.S. They reported in 1994 that 2.8% of the male, and 1.4% of the female, population identify themselves as gay, lesbian, or bisexual.[124] The 2000 U.S. Census counted gay men as 2% to 5% and lesbians from 1% to 3.5%, depending on how homosexuality was defined.[125] In 2011, Gary Gates, a demographer and Distinguished Scholar at The Williams Institute of UCLA School of Law, studied the studies and published his best estimate—4 million U.S. adults identify as being gay or lesbian, representing 1.7% of the adult population, or about 4 million people. By adding in bisexual, the number is 3.5% or 9 million people, a figure roughly equivalent to the population of New Jersey.[125.1]

The second myth is that homosexuality is developed in the womb but The Human Genome project identified all the genes in human DNA and found no homosexual gene existed (no transgender gene either).[126] In 1995, Scientific American issued what in effect was a retraction of two studies that were previously heralded by the press when they claimed the discovery of a "gay" gene. One study's results could not be replicated and in the other, the researcher "has been charged with research improprieties." In other words, he fudged his numbers.[127] Scientifically, to say that a gay gene causes homosexuality is not supported by DNA studies. No one is suggesting that homosexual feelings are invalid, just that no scientific findings support the idea that they are born that way. Therefore, homosexuality, like transgenderism, is far more likely to have been evolving during childhood development or perhaps even later in life.

The power of the activists to redefine truth is absolutely amazing. In the 1970s, they bullied the American Psychiatric Association (APA), publishers of the *Diagnostic Statistical Manual of Mental Disorders* (DSM), to remove homosexuality from the DSM. The DSM is the primary reference for medical professionals which defines mental illnesses and suggests current standards of treatment.

Activists are taking the next logical step to strengthen their political position and in the process, further deny transgenders access to psychological care. One activist web site promotes taking gender issues out of the DSM. They say this will allow transgenders to claim normalcy and thereby have a stronger position from which to lobby for civil rights legislation.[128]

The APA, to its credit, has appointed Dr. Kenneth Zucker as the chair of the work group for DSM-V Sexuality and Gender Identity Disorders. Zucker has an impressive resume as psychologist, professor, editor and researcher.[129] His research has a track record of following the medical evidence rather than the political winds.

The activists have bullied and lobbied the APA for years. In 2003, at a symposium sponsored by the APA, some mental health professionals proposed removing pedophilia, gender identity disorder, exhibitionism, fetishism, transvestism, voyeurism and sadomasochism from the DSM. A professional on the opposing side argued: "'Normalizing' pedophilia would have enormous implications, especially since civil laws closely follow the scientific community on social-moral matters." Another doctor shared the effect it would have on research: "Once you declassify it, there's no reason to continue studying it. [Declassification]...has a chilling effect on research."[130]

As a person who was subjected to frequent childhood molestations and abuses perpetrated by an adult, I say this: anyone who supports, engages in, or identifies with pedophilia in any way, shape or form is a very sick individual who should be put away. I find it appalling that anyone could even consider the decriminalization of child abuse. I will never in my lifetime be able to shake off the psychological effects of that childhood sexual abuse at the hands of my uncle.

Young kids are impressionable and as the brain research shows, early experiences shape them, in good ways or in harmful ways. We have the evidence of the tragic impact on Kinsey at age seven when he was playing with his young friends in one of the neighborhood basements:

> *According to biographer James Jones, about six kids played you show me and I'll show you. The children "look[ed] at one another, poke[d] straws in various apertures, stuff like that and that made him feel very peculiar and rather guilty." By age thirteen, Kinsey was a sex addict, highlighted by obsessive masturbation.[131]*

Like Kinsey found out in a neighborhood basement, behaviors are learned and reinforced through explicit life experience.

The activists are strongly supported by the American Civil Liberties Union (ACLU), which has a long history of defending abhorrent behavior in the name of liberty. The ACLU has defended the right of the pedophile organization NAMBLA (North American Man/Boy Love Association) to distribute child pornography.[132,133] The ACLU has pushed to abolish laws that would keep registered sex offenders away from our children and away from our schools.[134] Actions such as this make the ACLU, in my view, the most dangerous legal activist group in all of the United States. Never forget that the former president of the Virginia chapter of the ACLU was arrested for child pornography in 2007.[135]

From 1948 to the present day, it is safe to say Kinsey and the gender activists, powered by the ACLU, have done far more to advance changing genders and rework our nation's view of sexual behavior than all the presidents of the U.S., the hundreds of members of the Senate and the House of Representatives, the 200,000 church services held weekly[136], 954,000 U.S. doctors[137] and 93,000 psychologists[138] combined. We seem to be pushovers, not even putting up much of a fight, as if we are all hypnotized and brain dead. All the while, activists are redefining marriage and gender identity, and advancing pedophilia as normal.

Paul Newman and Robert Redford played train robbers as the characters of Butch Cassidy and the Sundance Kid in the 1969 film of the same name. In one of the most famous scenes, they joined hands and jumped from the big cliff into the unknown waters. When you have the GLBT social activists joining hands with the ACLU political and legal activists to jump off the cliff, they are taking an entire nation of three hundred million people with them into troubled waters. We are at the cliff's edge; do you really want to jump?

The activists use aggressive strong-arm tactics, by threatening reprisal towards any who do not agree with them. By now we all know the GLBT activists control the agenda, and that agenda is tolerance, diversity and political correctness. They effectively silence any other viewpoint by labeling it as intolerant. Tolerance, along with diversity, stands in the way of discovering any new effective psychological treatment for transgenders that will help prevent suicides.

I see it this way: the transgender activists want you to accept them as a discriminated, oppressed group. They say everyone is prejudiced against them and they face bigotry every day.[139] Transgenders whine that their civil rights are being denied, like those of blacks before the advent of the Civil Rights Movement. I find this to be a very shameful and unfortunate comparison. Blacks were relegated to poor housing and the back of the bus, and were hung by ropes in trees. Blacks simply wanted freedom to sit in a restaurant, take any seat on the bus, vote, and not live in fear for their lives. All very good reasons to want freedom and I'm happy these things changed where, even now, the President of the U.S.A. is black. Unlike our black brothers and sisters who are black at birth, transgenders were not born as transgenders; it took life experiences, hormones and a surgical procedure.

The truth is: transgenders are treated like rock stars. Movies and television shows glorify their life. They march in gay pride parades. Transgenders can sit in any restaurant, in fact they own many restaurants, and they can take any seat on the bus. They not only can vote, in fact, they are a very influential voting block. They go to the very best schools and universities in this country with freedom and protections in every state, but they want more, much more. They are redefining the very core of men, women and families.

As a former transgender myself who went on more than 200 job interviews without success, I always felt that employers had every right to discriminate and build the team of employees they want, not the ones the government wanted them to have. Discrimination is at the core of all we do all day long: where we live, cars we drive, food we eat and the people we associate with. I know people I wouldn't want to hang with and no government law should ever force me to do so. If people want to be non-conforming, fine with me, but they should know and expect some people will be repulsed.

The GLBT activists even have the power to bully President Barack Obama. In early 2011 in a victory for gay rights activists, the president declared that the 1996 federal law, the Defense of Marriage Act, which defines marriage as between a man and a woman, as unconstitutional.[140] This shows the power of GLBT activists to overturn federal law without even a vote or a court ruling, by controlling the occupant of the Oval Office. That is real power and influence. On a personal note, I have talked to some of my homosexual friends over the years who do not feel marriage is necessary and live just fine with their partners, but they are not activists.

Gender switchers are a part of the ongoing social scene. Unfortunately that scene includes too many misdiagnosed, depressed, suicidal, and dead by drug and alcohol abuse. I truly desire for transgenders to get the in-depth treatment they need to help prevent suicides and regret; the help I needed thirty years ago.

Contrary to the opinion of the advocates and their efforts to *eliminate* psychotherapy as part of transgender treatment, my suggestion is to *embrace* psychotherapy as part of a more comprehensive treatment plan. I fully understand my views will not resonate with everyone, but my voice will be a breath of fresh air to some, especially the ones who have known the torment and regret of gender surgery.

Summary

Throughout this book we discovered how for the last 100 years several major factors working together have shaped, advanced, and even controlled how our nation responds to each radical psychosurgery procedure and in every case advanced a medical practice which was largely a failure. The major factors working together are the media, the doctors, and those promoting an agenda. In earlier days the ones promoting an agenda were primarily the doctors with a self-promotion agenda. Today in the case of gender surgery, the activists are advancing a political agenda.

The media in the past, as well as today, has enormous power to influence society. They focus attention on anything that will attract an audience. For decades, the media has explored the novelty of gender surgery, selectively showing happy outcomes in headlines, films, and television. The media reports great success for transgenders and swallows the activist lie that regret occurs too rarely to even speak about. The media portrayals of success embolden the activists to do even more, knowing they can advance their agenda under the cover of the media. Meanwhile, 90% of transgenders are lost or unavailable for follow up, a critical mass that could spell disaster for the success rates, if publicized. The researchers have no idea if the 90% are dead, regret the surgery or if, like me, they have returned to their birth gender. But researchers completely downplay this reality and the media and activists willingly go along.

We've seen great illustrations of how media power and medical cover-up can help to perpetrate surgical fraud. Dr. Henry Cotton, who surgically removed teeth and colons to treat mental illness, skillfully manipulated the media, even as the majority of his patients were being maimed or killed. His powerful friend, Dr. Adolph Meyer buried a damaging study to protect his own reputation and that of his protégé, Dr. Cotton.

Dr. Walter Freeman, the ice pick doctor, perpetrator of the infamous lobotomy on adults and innocent children, was a showman who garnered intense media support with his unsubstantiated claims of curing mental illness. The truth is that for forty years he single-handedly turned low-functioning people into vacant-eyed mush, unable to care for themselves. The media was silent about the negative "side effects." His medical advocate, the same Dr. Adolph Meyer, influenced decades of lobotomy madness in order to promote his psychosurgery agenda.

Along came the media once again in 1966 shining the spotlight on Dr. John Money, a pedophile psychologist who, while he was on staff at Johns Hopkins University Gender Clinic, took pornographic pictures of his young patients, the Raimer twin boys. His powerful medical advocate was Dr. Harry Benjamin, who himself was inspired by Dr. Alfred Kinsey, a "violently masochistic masturbation addict" and a sexual predator.

Dr. Money experimented with the lives of the Raimer twins, persuading their parents to raise one as a girl and one as a boy. As a direct result of Money's treatment and abuse, one twin committed suicide; the other died from drug overdose. But first they revealed what Money had done to them in secret and how his treatment ruined their lives.

Dr. Money publicly claimed success with gender surgery, even though a ten-year follow-up study of the first gender surgeries at Johns Hopkins disputed his results and the program was shut down. He lied his way into becoming a media darling, and he unceasingly promoted surgery as the treatment for gender issues. Money was exposed as a fraud and a pedophile, but all too late.

The activists of the gay and lesbian movement embraced their friends, the transgenders, to further their shared political and social goals. The Gay, Lesbian, Bisexual, Transgender (GLBT) group became the new force behind gender surgery and it remains so today. The best way to grow political power is to grow the number of members. The GLBT activists would not let doctors and an objective study stand in the way of their agenda. They discounted the study and got into action, supporting everything and anything that would change even more lives through surgery. The transgender activists, small in number, have amassed an amazing amount of power thanks to the ACLU which provides the legal muscle to redefine the American family. The ACLU, through persistence in the courts, has exerted tremendous influence over our lawmakers, school curriculum, and the socialization of transgenders, and we have shown how they seek out cases that will further the GLBT agenda.

I think it is amazing that the agenda to break down societal taboos started by Kinsey using suspect research, and then taken up by like-minded GLBT activists, has gathered the power to generate so many laws protecting one group of people because they engage in sex differently. This is the very same group of people that will not use a condom to protect themselves or even their sex partners from HIV/AIDS. But they want the federal government (we the taxpayers) to cover the costs for HIV/AIDS treatments and to pay for gender surgery, even if they are serving a life sentence for murder. This is astonishing; they have bamboozled everyone into thinking they are the victims.

We as a society have become so accustomed to looking the other way when confronted with lies, that we become the living fabric of the lies. When the truth is inconvenient, we just exclude it. When facts get in the way, we make up our own. No matter how absurd or foolish the argument, even when faced with overwhelming objective evidence to the contrary, we swallow the lie.

We as a society have become so damn politically correct in the pursuit of tolerance, that if we should happen to acknowledge to ourselves the truth, we are intimidated into silence, not willing to risk being called intolerant or more colorful names to that effect. We say nothing, as if the real truth has no place in the pursuit of genuine medical treatment based on sound, robust research. We only shake our heads at the foolishness that surrounds us; no one will stand up and fight.

The activists will continue to have their way and will remain undaunted by the deaths and failures, but this book, *Paper Genders*, pulls the mask off so you can see the truth of sorrow, regret and failure. So many who have undergone gender surgery are silent, unable to shout out the truth of their situation, that the surgery made things worse or they want their old gender back. Sadly, many are hiding out in shame at their foolishness, or are covered by grass and headstones, lying in their graves.

This is why I'm taking this opportunity to speak out. I was one of the 90% who were once lost and could not be counted among the success stories. The statistics of suicides, substance abuse, and self-mutilation, joined with the personal testimonies make a strong case that surgery is not a universally effective treatment for gender disorders.

We have shown evidence of media, doctors, and advocates working in concert to promote only the success of gender change. They continue to hide the truth about failures and boast about amazing surgical success. I feel we need to care more about the needlessly lost lives and truly provide effective treatment for individuals who struggle with gender identity. Effective treatment can start by treating co-existing psychological disorders, making improvements in the surgery approval process, and providing care that may not include surgery. That is the least we can do.

The mask is off.

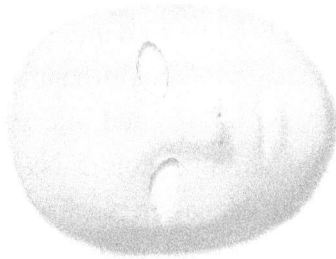

End Notes

❦

CHAPTER 1

1   UCSB SexInfoOnline, "Intersex," downloaded on March 20, 2011 from http://www.soc.ucsb.edu/sexinfo/article/intersex

2   Clara Moskowitz, "Transgender Americans face high suicide risk / New survey paints a portrait of trans people's lives in the U.S.," LiveScience, updated November 19, 2010, downloaded on March 22, 2011 from http://www.msnbc.msn.com/id/40279043/ns/health-health_care/

3   Laura Amato, "Transgender Mortality Rate: Suicide, Medical, Violence," downloaded on March 22, 2011 from http://www.lauras-playground.com/transgender_mortality.htm

4   Laura Amato

5   TGLynnsPlace.com, "Transgender Suicide," downloaded on March 22, 2011 from *http://www.tglynnsplace.com/suicide.htm*

6   Roger Chapman, *Culture wars: an encyclopedia of issues, viewpoints, and voices, Volume 1*, (M.E. Sharpe, 2010), 302

7   William F. Jasper, senior editor of *The New American*, "Fighting the Kinsey Fraud / Interview with Dr. Judith Reisman," posted by Wes Penre, May 26, 2005, downloaded on February 26, 2011 from http://

www.illuminati-news.com/alfred-kinsey2.htm

8　　　Judith A. Reisman, Ph.D., *Sexual Sabotage*, (WND Books, 2010), 36

9　　　Judith A. Reisman, *Sexual Sabotage*, 36, 43, 158

10　　Paul Likoudis, "The Real Expert Advises Bishops: Sue Your Experts," *The Wanderer*, interview with Dr. Judith Reisman, downloaded on February 26, 2011 from http://www.drjudithreisman.com/letters.html

11　　William F. Jasper, "Fighting the Kinsey Fraud / Interview with Dr. Judith Reisman"

12　　Erwin J. Haeberle, "The Transatlantic Commuter, an interview with Harry Benjamin (b. January 12, 1885) on the occasion of his 100th birthday," *Archive for Sexology*, published in "Sexualmedizin," vol. 14, 1/1985, downloaded on March 15, 2011 from http://www2.hu-berlin.de/sexology/GESUND/ARCHIV/ TRANS_B5.HTM

13　　Judith Reisman, *Kinsey: Crimes and Consequences*, (Inst for Media Education, 1998), 220

14　　Judith A. Reisman, *Kinsey: Crimes and Consequences*, 189, 222

15　　Wikipedia, "Harry Benjamin," downloaded on February 1, 2011 from http://en.wikipedia.org/wiki/Harry_Benjamin

16　　Paul Likoudis, "The real expert advises bishops: Sue your experts"

17　　"Sexes: Attacking the Last Taboo," *Time Magazine*, April 14, 1980, downloaded on March 15, 2011 from http://www.time.com/time/magazine/article/0,9171,923966,00.html

18　　Joseph Geraci and Donald Mader, "Interview: John Money," *PAIDIKA: The Journal of Paedophilia*, Spring 1991, vol. 2, no. 3, p. 5

19　　Judith A. Reisman, *Kinsey: Crimes and Consequences*, 82

20　　Laura Wexler, "Identity Crisis," Style Magazine, *The Baltimore Sun*, January/February 2007, downloaded on Feb. 18, 2011 from http://www.baltimorestyle.com/index.php/style/features_article/fe_sexchange_jf07/

21　　Laura Wexler, "Identity Crisis"

22　　John Money, "Prefatory remarks on outcome of sex reassignment in

24 cases of transsexualism," *Archives Of Sexual Behavior,* Volume 1, Number 2, 163-165

23   BBC, "Dr. Money and the Boy with No Penis/Programme transcript"

24   Laura Wexler, "Identity Crisis"

25   Jon K. Meyer, MD and Donna J. Reter , "Sex reassignment. Follow-up" *Archives of General Psychiatry,* 1979;36(9):1010-1015

26   Paul McHugh. "Surgical Sex" *First Things*, 147 (November 2004): 34-38.

27   Laura Wexler, "Identity Crisis"

28   Pauline Arrillaga, "Sex change nickname makes Colo. town cringe: 'Nobody cares' Transformation via surgery has become common in community, " *The Associated Press*, appeared in *USA Today*, May 24, 2000, 4A

29   Margalit Fox, "Stanley H. Biber, 82, Surgeon Among First to Do Sex Changes, Dies, " *The New York Times*, January 21, 2006

30   Erwin J. Haeberle, "The Transatlantic Commuter, An interview with Harry Benjamin (b. January 12, 1885) on the occasion of his 100th birthday"

31   Kevin Spak, "Transgender Sportswriter's Suicide Leaves Questions, Why did Christine Daniels turn back into Mike Penner?," *Newser*, posted Dec. 1, 2009, downloaded on February 10, 2011 from http://www.newser.com/story/75115/transgender-sportswriters-suicide-leaves-questions.html

32   Randi Ettner, Stan Monstrey, A. Evan Eyler, editors, *Principles of transgender medicine and surgery,* (The Haworth Press, 2007), Chapter 5: Surgery: general principles by Stan Monstrey, Griet De Cuypere, Randi Ettner, 96

33   Lauras-Playground.com, "Transgender, Transsexual, Peers Wanted for Suicide Prevention Help," Downloaded on February 1, 2011 from http://www.lauras-playground.com/transgender_peers_suicide.htm

CHAPTER 2

34   Pagan Kennedy, *The Boston Globe*, "Q&A with Norman Spack, A doctor helps children change their gender," boston.com, March 30, 2008

34.1   Gudrun Schultz, "Boston Children's Hospital Opens "Transgender" Children's Clinic," lifesitenews.com, downloaded on April 7, 2011 from http://www.lifesitenews.com/news/archive/ldn/2007/may/07051806

35   Tracy Jan, *The Boston Globe*, "Methuen school faces parents' queries on student's gender issue / Officials back girl who seeks treatment as boy," boston.com, March 5, 2005, downloaded on February 16, 2011 from http://www.boston.com/news/local/articles/2005/03/05/ methuen_ school_faces_parents_queries_on_students_gender_issue/

36   Bob Unruh, "Lawmakers pass redefinition of 'sex' / Bill threatens references to 'mom,' 'dad' at school," WorldNetDaily.com, May 24, 2007

37   Peter Singer, *Rethinking Life and Death,* Macmillan, 1996, p.217

38   William J. Federer, "Auschwitz in America," WorldNetDaily.com, October 18, 2003

39   *The Washington Times*, "EDITORIAL: Obama's risky-sex czar," December 9, 2009

40   Angela Wilson, "Is Kevin Jennings the best person to be the Safe Schools Czar?" Examiner.com, December 15, 2009

41   Jim Hoft, "Breaking: Obama's "Safe Schools Czar" Is Promoting Child Porn in the Classroom– Kevin Jennings and the GLSEN Reading List," rightnetwork.com, December 4, 2009

42   Angela Wilson

43   *The Washington Times*, "EDITORIAL: Obama's risky-sex czar," December 9, 2009

44   Denene Millner, "Holy hormones! What to expect when puberty hits," CNN Health, April 1, 2009

45   Joost à Campo, M.D., Henk Nijman, Ph.D., H. Merckelbach, Ph.D., and Catharine Evers, M.Sc., "Psychiatric Comorbidity of Gender Identity Disorders: A Survey Among Dutch Psychiatrists," *Am J Psychiatry*

160:1332-1336, July 2003

46 Joost à Campo, 1332-1336

47 Joost à Campo, 1332

48 Joost à Campo, 1332

49 Anne Vitale, Editor, Notes on Gender Role Transition, T-Note 15, "Testosterone Toxicity Implicated in Male-To-Female Transsexuals? Some thoughts," March 21, 2009, downloaded on February 2, 2011 from http://www.avitale.com/TNote15Testosterone.htm

50 "Poilievre seeks ban on funding for sex change surgery in Ontario / Conservative MP Pierre Poilievre says he wants the federal government to step in and prevent Ontario from funding sex reassignment surgery" *The Ottawa Citizen*, May 20, 2008, downloaded on February 2, 2011 from http://www.canada.com/ottawacitizen/news/story. html?id=1fa084fb-359a-41ad-9213-4205992e7eb6

51 "Adolescent Brain Development and Legal Culpability," January 2004, American Bar Association, Juvenile Justice Center, downloaded on February 3, 2011 from http://www.abanet.org/crimjust/juvjus/ Adolescence.pdf

52 "Inside the Teenage Brain," PBS *Frontline* program, program #2011, original airdate January 31, 2002, written, produced and directed by Sarah Spinks, transcript downloaded on March 23, 2011 from http:// www.pbs.org/wgbh/pages/frontline/shows/teenbrain/etc/script.html

53 Keith Ferrell, "What's Going On in the Teenage Brain?," Healthy Children Magazine, Fall 2007

54 Tracy Jan, *The Boston Globe*

55 *How Are the Children? Report on Early Childhood Development and Learning,* U.S. Department of Education, September 1999, http://www2. ed.gov/pubs/How_Children/index.html

56 *How Are the Children? Report on Early Childhood Development and Learning,* U.S. Department of Education

57 Susan D. Witt, Ph.D , "Parental Influence on Children's Socialization to Gender Roles," *Adolescence*, Summer, 1997, downloaded from http:// gozips.uakron.edu/~susan8/parinf.htm

58 American Foundation for Suicide Prevention, "Risk Factors for Suicide," downloaded on March 6, 2011 from http://www.afsp.org/index. cfm?page_id=05147440-E24E-E376-BDF4BF8BA6444E76

59 Jaime M. Grant, Ph.D., Lisa A. Mottet, J.D., and Justin Tanis, D.Min. With Jody L. Herman, Ph.D., Jack Harrison, and Mara Keisling, "National Transgender Discrimination Survey Report on health and health care / Findings of a Study by the National Center for Transgender Equality and the National Gay and Lesbian Task Force," October 2010, 14, downloaded on March 23, 2011 from http://www.thetaskforce.org/ downloads/reports/reports/ntds_report_on_health.pdf

60 Clara Moskowitz, "High Suicide Risk, Prejudice Plague Transgender People," LiveScience, November 19, 2010, downloaded on February 2, 2011 from http://www.livescience.com/culture/transgender-mental-health-suicide--101119.html

CHAPTER 3

61 *The George Washington University and Foggy Bottom Historical Encyclopedia*, "Freeman, Walter," downloaded on February 15, 2011 from http://encyclopedia.gwu.edu/gwencyclopedia/index. php?title=Freeman%2C_Walter

62 Andrew T. Scull, *Madhouse: A Tragic Tale of Megalomania and Modern Medicine*, (Yale University Press, 2005), 286-287

63 Asylum Projects, downloaded on February 14, 2011 from http://www. asylumprojects.org/index.php?title=Walter_Freeman

64 *The George Washington University and Foggy Bottom Historical Encyclopedia*, "Freeman, Walter"

65 Laurence Leamer, *The Kennedy Women: The Saga of an American Family,* (Villard Books, a division of Random House, 1994), 138

66 Leamer, 322

67 Peter Collier, David Horowitz, *The Kennedys: An American Drama,* (Encounter Books, 2002), 400

68 Renato M.E. Sabbatini, Ph.D., *Lobotomy's Hall of Fame,* downloaded on February 8, 2011 from http://www.cerebromente.org.br/n02/historia/ important.htm

69   Mel Gussow, *Rose Williams, 86, Sister And the Muse of Playwright*, New York Times, September 07, 1996, downloaded on February 8, 2011 from http://www.nytimes.com/1996/09/07/arts/rose-williams-86-sister-and-the-muse-of-playwright.html

70   *The George Washington University and Foggy Bottom Historical Encyclopedia*, "Freeman, Walter"

71   Samuel Greenblatt, T. Dagi, and Mel Epstein, *A History of Neurosurgery: In its Scientific and Professional Contexts,* (Thieme Medical Publishers, 1997), 510

72   Kelly Patricia O'Meara, "Forgotten Dead of St. Elizabeth's," *Insight Magazine*, July 2001, downloaded on February 8, 2011 from http://www.recoveryxchange.org/downloads/Forgotten%20Dead%20of%20St.%20Elizabeth%27s.pdf

73   *The Lobotomist*, An Ark Media film for American Experience, 2008 WGBH Educational Foundation, Produced and Directed by Barak Goodman and John Maggio, downloaded on February 8, 2011 from http://www.pbs.org/wgbh/americanexperience/features/transcript/lobotomist-transcript/

74   Andrew T. Scull, *The insanity of place, the place of insanity: essays on the history of psychiatry*, (Taylor & Francis, 2006), 135

75   Jack El-Hai, "The Lobotomist," Special to *The Washington Post* Sunday, February 4, 2001; Page W16 downloaded on February 1, 2011 from http://www.washingtonpost.com/ac2/wp-dyn?pagename=article&node=&contentId=A4531-2001Jan30

76   Jack El-Hai, *The lobotomist: a maverick medical genius and his tragic quest to rid the world of mental illness*, (J. Wiley, 2005), 171

77   Clinton C. Brown, "Head Hunters," PsycCRITIQUES – Feb 1, 1957, Volume 2 (2): 47, downloaded on February 18, 2011 from http://mcs-dd.sagepub.com/lp/psyccritiques-reg/head-hunters-h41fN9Jt5w

78   Renato M.E. Sabbatini, Ph.D., "The History of Psychosurgery," *Brain and Mind Magazine*, Number 2: June-August, 1997, downloaded on February 9, 2011 from http://www.cerebromente.org.br/n02/historia/psicocirg_i.htm

79   Katherine A. Kean, Times Record/Roane County Reporter, West Virginia Archives and History, *Spencer State Hospital, State Hospital story began*

on a note of hope, July 6, 1989, downloaded on February 18, 2011 from http://www.wvculture.org/history/government/spencer03.html

80   Katherine A. Kean

81   Downloaded on February 18, 2011 from http://quotedepot.net/famous-people/friedrich-hegel/20150/quotes

82   Laura Wexler, *Identity Crisis*

83   Andrew T. Scull, *Madhouse: A Tragic Tale of Megalomania and Modern Medicine*, (Yale University Press, 2005), 286-287

84   "Mass lobotomies," *Time Magazine*, Vol. 60, no. 11, September 15, 1952, 86-87

85   Howard Dully and Charles Fleming, *My Lobotomy, A Memoir,* (Random House, 2007)

86   A. Chris Gajilan, "Survivor recounts lobotomy at age 12, Procedure once considered legitimate medical treatment," CNN, Thursday, December 1, 2005, downloaded on February 14, 2011 from http://edition.cnn.com/2005/HEALTH/conditions/11/30/pdg.lobotomy/index.html

87   A. Chris Gajilan

88   Howard Dully and Charles Fleming, *My Lobotomy: A Memoir*, 268

89   Howard Dully and Charles Fleming, *My Lobotomy: A Memoir*

90   Albert Ellis, Mike Abrams, Lidia Dengelegi Abrams, *Personality theories: critical perspectives,* (SAGE, 2008), 178

91   Jack El-Hai, *The lobotomist: a maverick medical genius and his tragic quest to rid the world of mental illness*, (J. Wiley, 2005), 1

92   Sarah E. Richards, "Neurostimulation / Is it a good idea to drill holes in people's heads to treat them for depression?," Tuesday, February 19, 2008, Slate.com, downloaded on February 19, 2011 from http://www.slate.com/id/2184699/

93   A. Chris Gajilan

CHAPTER 4

94   Andrew Scull, *Madhouse: A Tragic Tale of Megalomania and Modern Medicine*, (Yale University Press, 2005), 53-55

95   Hugh Freeman, "Infectious lunacy," A review of "Madhouse: A Tragic Tale of Megalomania and Modern Medicine" by Andrew Scull, appeared in *The Times Literary Supplement*, Sunday, September 18th, 2005, downloaded on February 24, 2011 from http://www.powells.com/review/2005_09_18.html

96   Andrew Scull, 54-55

97   Andrew Scull, 181

98   Andrew Scull, 278

99   Andrew Scull, 69

100   Andrew Scull, 65

101   Thomas Quinn Beesley, "When the Brain Is Sick" (A Review of "The Defective, Delinquent and Insane" by Henry A. Cotton, M. D.), *The New York Times*, June 18, 1922, Section *The New York Times Book Review*, Page 56, downloaded on February 23, 2011 from http://query.nytimes.com/mem/archive-free/pdf?res=F50F16FE3B5D14738DDDA10994DE405B828EF1D3

102   Michael Nevins, *A Tale of Two Villages: Vineland and Skillman, NJ*, (iUniverse, 2009)

103   Michael Nevins, 9

104   Hugh Freeman, "Infectious lunacy"

105   Andrew Scull, 338

106   Andrew Scull, 297

CHAPTER 5

107   Group Insurance Concepts, *Insurance Glossary*, downloaded on February 27, 2011 from http://www.myinsuranceguy.com/glossary3. htm

108 "Mass. inmate asks for sex change," posted 6/26/2007 2:45 PM on *USAToday.com*, Copyright 2007 The Associated Press, downloaded on February 28, 2011 from http://www.usatoday.com/news/nation/2007-06-26-inmate-sex change_N.htm

109 "Mass. inmate asks for sex change," posted 6/26/2007 2:45 PM on *USAToday.com*, Copyright 2007 The Associated Press

110 Kenly Walker, "Inmate's Sex change Request Draws Scrutiny," CBS News, downloaded on February 27, 2011 from http://www. cbsnews. com/stories/2007/06/26/national/main2983479.shtm

111 Bruce Vielmetti, "Sex change drugs a right, judge says / State law limiting inmates overruled," *Journal Sentinel*, April 1, 2010, downloaded on February 28, 2011 from http://www.jsonline.com/news/wisconsin/89701297.html

112 Bruce Vielmetti

113 Kathleen Harris, QMI Agency, "Prison system grapples with transgendered inmates / Sex-switch surgery funded for offenders, but not for all Canadians," downloaded on February 28, 2011 from http://cnews. canoe.ca/CNEWS/Canada/2010/11/19/16228256.html

114 Downloaded on March 6, 2011 from http://gbge.aclu.org/transgender

115 Downloaded on March 6, 2011 from http://transgriot.blogspot. com/2008/11/monicas-transcending-gender-keynote.html

116 Althea Chang, "Unusual perks: Goldman Sachs covers sex changes," *Fortune*, February 8, 2008, downloaded on March 1, 2011 from http://money.cnn.com/2008/02/08/news/companies/ gender.fortune/index.htm

117 Christine Hogan, "Man who became woman wants to be a man again," The Sun-Herald, August 31, 2003, downloaded on March 1, 2011 from http://www.smh.com.au/articles/2003/08/30/ 1062194756832.html

118 Joost à Campo, M.D., Henk Nijman, Ph.D., H. Merckelbach, Ph.D., and Catharine Evers, M.Sc., Psychiatric Comorbidity of Gender Identity Disorders: A Survey Among Dutch Psychiatrists, Am J Psychiatry 160:1332-1336, July 2003

119 Madeleine Wallien, Hanna Swaab, Peggy Cohen-Kettenis, "Psychiatric Comorbidity Among Children With Gender Identity Disorder," J Am Acad Child Adolesc Psychiatry, 2007 Oct ;46 (10):1307-1314

17885572 Cit:7, downloaded on March 1, 2011 from http://lib.bioinfo.pl/pmid:17885572

120   Jeffrey Herbst, Elizabeth Jacobs, Teresa Finlayson, Vel McKleroy, Mary Neumann, Nicole Crepaz, "Estimating HIV Prevalence and Risk Behaviors of Transgender Persons in the United States: A Systematic Review," AIDS Behav. 2007 Aug 13, downloaded on March 3, 2011 from http://lib.bioinfo.pl/pmid:17694429

121   Dana G. Finnegan, Emily B. McNally, Counseling lesbian, gay, bisexual, and transgender substance, (Psychology Press, 2002), 55 The full quote is: "Valentine's study (1998) of intake records at the Gender Identity Project in New York City showed high rates of substance abuse in the transgender population: 27. 1 percent reported alcohol abuse; 23.6 percent reported drug abuse."

CHAPTER 6

122   Judith A. Reisman, *Sexual Sabotage*, 36

123   Bruce Voeller, "Some uses and abuses of the Kinsey scale" in D.P. McWhirter, S.A. Sanders, & J.M. Reinisch (Eds.), *Homosexuality/heterosexuality: Concepts of sexual orientation*, (New York: Oxford University Press, 1990), 32-38

124   Edward O. Laumann, John H. Gagnon, Robert T. Michael, Stuart Michaels, *The Social Organization of Sex: Sexual Practices in the United States*, (University of Chicago Press, 2000)

125   Allison Tarmann, "Out of the Closet and Onto the Census Long Form," *Population Today*, May/June 2002, downloaded on April 5, 2011 from Population Reference Bureau at http://www.prb.org/Articles/2002/OutoftheClosetandOntotheCensusLongForm.aspx?p=1

125.1 Gary J. Gates, Williams Distinguished Scholar, "How many people are lesbian, gay, bisexual, and transgender?", The Williams Institute, UCLA School of Law, April 2011, downloaded from http://www2.law.ucla.edu/williamsinstitute/pdf/How-many-people-are-LGBT-Final.pdf

126   Dr. Brad Harrub, Dr. Bert Thompson and Dr. Dave Miller, "A Scientific Examination of Homosexuality and the 'Gay Gene,'" The True Origin Archive, (2003), http://www.azconservative.org/page12.php

127   John Horgan, "Gay Genes, Revisited," Scientific American Magazine,

November 1995

128   Downloaded on March 12, 2011 from http://www.change.org/petitions/
       remove_transgender_from_the_dsm-5#?opt_new=t

129   American Psychiatric Association, downloaded on March 12, 2011
       from http://www.psych.org/MainMenu/Research/DSMIV/DSMV/
       MeettheTaskForce/KennethJZuckerPhD.aspx

       "Dr. Zucker is Psychologist-in-Chief at the Centre for Addiction and
       Mental Health (CAMH) and is the Head of the Gender Identity Service
       in the Child, Youth, and Family Program at CAMH. He is a Professor
       in the Departments of Psychiatry and Psychology at the University of
       Toronto and holds cross-appointments at the Hospital for Sick Children,
       the Ontario Institute for Studies in Education of the University of
       Toronto, and York University. He has been the Editor of *Archives of
       Sexual Behavior* since 2002 and is a Past President of the International
       Academy of Sex Research. Dr. Zucker's research interests pertain to the
       development of psychosexual differentiation and its disorders. He has
       conducted a variety of studies pertaining to gender identity disorder in
       children, including diagnosis and assessment, cross-national comparative
       studies, associated psychopathology, tests of etiological hypotheses, and
       long-term follow-up. He also conducts research in the area of disorders
       of sex development (physical intersex conditions)."

130   Lawrence Morahan, CNSnews.com Senior Staff Writer, "Psychiatric
       Association Debates Reclassifying Pedophilia," June 11, 2003,
       downloaded on March 12, 2011 from http://www.canadiancrc.
       com/Newspaper_Articles/CNS_ABA_Debates_Reclassifying_
       Pedo_11JUN03.aspx

131   Judith A. Reisman, *Sexual Sabotage*, 36-37

132   Deroy Murdock, "No Boy Scouts, The ACLU defends NAMBLA,"
       National Review Online, February 27, 2004, downloaded on
       March 12, 2011 from http://old.nationalreview.com/murdock/
       murdock200402270920.asp

133   Associated Press, "ACLU to Defend Pedophile Group," August 31,
       2000, downloaded on March 12, 2011 from http://www.wired.com/
       politics/law/news/2000/08/38540

134   Clynton Namuo, "NHCLU sues Dover over sex-offender restrictions,"
       March 27, 2008, UnionLeader.com, downloaded on March 12, 2011
       from http://www.unionleader.com/article.aspx? articleId=a366fb7f-bf10-

401c-8d91-73134da911de&headline= NHCLU+sues+Dover+over+sex-offender+restrictions

135 Jack Date, "Former ACLU Chapter President Arrested for Child Pornography, Complaint Alleges Virginia Man Accessed, Downloaded Graphic Child Pornography," ABCnews.com, Feb. 23, 2007, downloaded on March 12, 2011 from http://abcnews.go.com/Politics/story?id=2900174&page=1

136 Christopher Enstad, WorkingPreacher.org, a review of David T. Olson's *The American Church in Crisis: groundbreaking research based on a national database of over 200,000 churches.* (Grand Rapids, Mich.: Zondervan, 2008), posted June 30, 2010, downloaded on March 12, 2011 from http://www.workingpreacher.org/chartingculture.aspx?article_id=369

137 Suzanne Sataline and Shirley S. Wang, "Medical Schools Can't Keep Up," *The Wall Street Journal*, April 12, 2010, downloaded on March 12, 2011 from http://online.wsj.com/article/ SB10001424052702304506904575180331528424238.html

138 American Psychological Association, downloaded on March 12, 2011 from http://www.apa.org/support/about/psych/numbers-us.aspx#answer

139 David Crary, "Transgender activists face multiple challenges," Associated Press, Feb. 4, 2011 downloaded on March 12, 2011 from http://news.yahoo.com/s/ap/20110204/ap_on_re_us/us_transgender_rights

140 CNN Wire Staff, "Obama administration won't oppose same-sex marriage," CNN.com, February 23, 2011 downloaded on March 12, 2011 from http://www.cnn.com/2011/POLITICS/02/23/obama.gay.marriage/

Online Sources of Information

www.WaltHeyer.com

www.SexChangeRegret.com

 confo

Contact the Author

waltsbook@yahoo.com

More Books *by* Walt Heyer

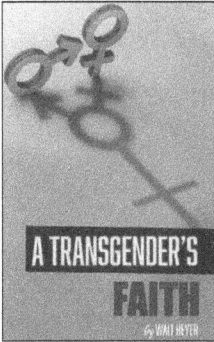

A Transgender's Faith

Walt's story
"…a true miracle story…
about a very personal and
powerful struggle…"

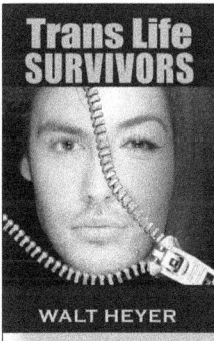

Trans Life Survivors

30 stories powerfully portray
the human toll caused by
gender change.

Includes the latest research
and a special section on
children.

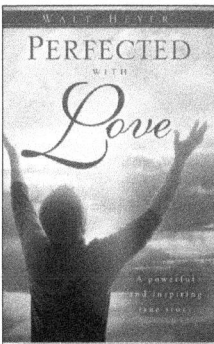

Perfected with Love

"a powerful story…
that teaches about the radical
nature of love in action."

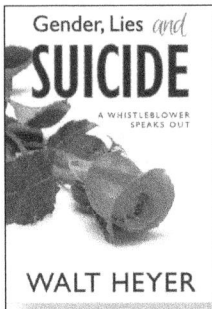

www.ingramcontent.com/pod-product-compliance
Lightning Source LLC
Chambersburg PA
CBHW030253030426
42336CB00009B/368